Why Church Matters

Worship, Ministry, and Mission in Practice

Jonathan R. Wilson

Published by Brazos Press
a division of Baker Publishing Group
P.O. Box 6287, Grand Rapids, MI 49516-6287
www.brazospress.com

Printed in the United States of America

Library of Congress Cataloging-in-Publication Data
Wilson, Jonathan R.
    Why church matters : worship, ministry, and mission in practice /
Jonathan R. Wilson
        p.   cm.
    Includes bibliographical references and index.
    ISBN 10: 1-58743-037-1 (pbk.)
    ISBN 978-1-58743-037-4 (pbk.)
    1. Church. I. Title
BV600.3.W57 2006
262—dc22   2006017095

Contents

Preface

Why does church matter? Because "church" names the people of God who make known God's love for the world in Jesus Christ through the work of the Holy Spirit. "Why Church Matters" gets to the heart of the book, but my working title was "Practicing Church." By "practicing church" I primarily mean that since the love of God in Christ is actively at work in the world, the witness of the church simply is its participation in that work of God. The notion of practice, as I develop and apply it in this book, illuminates God's redemptive work and further enables the church's witness to that work.

So this book is about "practicing church" as the formation of a people whose life together witnesses to God's redemption of creation. God accomplishes that redemption in, for, and through Jesus Christ. Witness to that redemption is possible only in a community sustained by the power of the Holy Spirit. The community that lives the way of Jesus is the church, the disciple community. Sometimes we witness to Jesus Christ by faithfully living out the gospel. Sometimes, when we live unfaithfully, we bear witness to Jesus Christ by bearing God's judgment before the world, by confessing our sin, by turning to God's gracious forgiveness, which the whole world needs.

This book is written to enable greater faithfulness in the way of Jesus Christ and to enable confession and forgiveness in the midst of unfaithfulness. To accomplish this, I focus closely on a notion of "practice" that goes beyond "just do it." The first chapter explains this notion of practice, which guides the following chapters. Those following chapters are divided among three sections. The first section attends to practices that generate and sustain the life of the church. The second section addresses practices that I judge to be particularly in need of renovation. The third section addresses practices that build upon the foundations and renovations of the previous chapters. In this third section I have deliberately used imagery of formation rather than construction to remind us that while the church is often described in the New Testament as a building, that imagery is complemented by language that describes the church as an organism—the body of Christ.

In this book I intend to give a relatively comprehensive account of the practices of the church: the role of the pastor, the proclamation of the gospel, the celebration of the sacraments, worship, evangelism, discipline, and many more activities are developed as practices. Certainly none of these may be reduced to a practice; each is much more. But examining each as a practice opens up many new ways of understanding and living out these activities. At first glance, these practices may seem to be concerned primarily with the "inward" life of the church—what forms and sustains the life of the church rather than what carries its mission into the world. However, I am convinced that the distinction between inward and outward, while helpful, may also mislead us. The (inward) life of the church is its (outward) mission, and the mission of the church is its life. In the following chapters I give an account of the life of the church as its mission.

This work is shaped by many years as a pastor's son, keenly aware of the life of the church and the ways that its life can go wrong. It is shaped by years as an occasional confidant of my pastors, especially George Lee and Milton Worthington. It is significantly shaped by an informal but thorough apprenticeship under Roy Bell at First Baptist Church, Vancouver, and formal mentoring under Don Anderson. My three years as a part-time hospital chaplain gave me another angle of vision on the church and others' perception of it. My own pastorate at Edmonds Baptist Church (1980–1986) forced me to seek some ways of thinking and leading that could help a congregation recover its identity and mission. My doctoral studies at Duke provided me with a more refined understanding of practice that I have developed in my own writing and ministry. Since Duke, I have been discipled by the life of Montecito Covenant Church, Santa Barbara Community Church, and Kentville United Baptist Church.

This book is dedicated to my wife, whose impatience with the church and patient practice of prayer contribute far more to the church's faithfulness than anything I may write. I want also to acknowledge the example of Rutba House, the Christian community in the Walltown Neighborhood of Durham, North Carolina, where our daughter, Leah, and son-in-law, Jonathan, live and practice the good news of Jesus Christ with many others.

Part One

Foundations

1

On Practice and Practical Theology

*W*hy do American teenagers get up before dawn during certain times of the year, travel to large buildings with high ceilings, sprint between lines on the floor until they are gasping, bounce and throw orange orbs inflated with air, and run intricate patterns around one another, while an adult shouts instructions, yells corrections, and occasionally pierces the air with a shrill whistle? Because they are all committed to basketball, of course. The sacrifices of these teenagers and their parents make sense only if their actions are directed toward being better at basketball.

Why do millions of Americans (and others all around the world) of all ages get up a little earlier than necessary each morning, read from translations of texts that are two to three thousand years old, praise and petition God, gather together on their day off from work and school, sing to God, confess their sins, celebrate their forgiveness, give money, listen to a sermon, eat small portions of bread, and drink small portions of wine? Because they are the church, of course.

The church does those things, but I don't think that we who are the church have a clear sense of what it is that we are to do *as the church* or why we do those things *as the church*. In this book I hope to give a clear description of what it is that we are called to do as the church and a compelling account of why we do those things. By so doing, I hope also to help us discern when we are being faithful and when we are being unfaithful.

To begin to think about the activities of the church as practices that matter, we must go beyond the standard questions that we wrestle with and think about why these activities matter to the church's participation in God's redemptive work. As an example (to which we will return later), consider the significance of the church's celebration of Communion. Of course, one can distinguish among the church traditions by asking certain questions about Communion. Who may participate? Who may administer Communion? What is understood to happen to the bread and the wine? What is the relationship between this act and salvation? But I am asking another question: what does the celebration of Communion signify for the life of the church?

For example, does the church understand that Communion is God's act of hospitality in which God as host welcomes us to the dinner table? Does that question even make sense in our various congregations? If so, is there a clear and consistent answer to it or at least careful reflection on it? Is Communion as God's act of hospitality lived out in the way it is celebrated? Does the congregation understand and live out hospitality in their own life together and with the world? Is that living out shaped by Communion?

These are the kinds of questions, asked across the whole range of the church's life, that shape this book. To ask and answer these questions I will deploy a notion of "practice" that has been developed recently in a number of different works. Thus I am concerned with "the practicing church," not because I think that the church is rehearsing for the real thing to come later but because I think that the church is constituted as God's people by its practices. These practices constitute the church because it is called by God to bear witness to the good news of Jesus Christ.

At the end of his analysis of secularization, Julian Hartt concludes that "secularity at its best is . . . a powerful rebuke to Christians living in bad faith. But the proper response to such a rebuke is not to abandon the Christian faith. It would be better to practice it."[1]

---

1. Julian N. Hartt, *The Restless Quest* (Philadelphia: United Church Press, 1975), 113.

This book is written under the conviction that Hartt's call to practice is even more significant today than when he first issued it. The significance of "practice" for the life of the church is rooted in two convictions, one about the gospel and the other about our present circumstances.

First, I am convinced, with many others, that the good news of Jesus Christ is fundamentally not a set of ideas or system of belief but the grace of God made known in human lives. The church is the body of people who believe the good news and are chosen by God to bear witness to it. The church's witness bearing is testimony not to its own life but *to God's grace in its life*. Since that grace is the good news of Jesus Christ, it bears witness to the entire history of Christ's coming, including his continuing work through the Holy Spirit in the power of his resurrection.[2] That grace of the gospel is both judgment and redemption. The judgment of grace reveals our sin, so that we may confess, repent, and be forgiven. The redemption of grace is the transformation of our lives into a new people. Thus, the good news to which the church is called as witness is fundamentally a way of life. It must be "acted out"; it must be practiced.

The second conviction that guides my concern with practice is our present circumstances. I am convinced that the greatest threat to the faithful witness bearing of the church is the absence of vibrant and vital practices of the gospel. When the life of the church is alive with practices faithful to the gospel, the witness of the church simply has to point to those practices. "You want to know what the love [mercy, grace, forgiveness] of Christ means? Well, take a look at *that* relationship" or "that congregation." In times of vibrancy, the church has little need of a verbal argument for the truth of the gospel; instead its argument is found in the practice of the gospel, the presence of grace in the life of the church.

In the absence of such vibrancy, the church becomes more wordy, seeking to substitute explanation and argument for faithful practice. Or the church longs for and frantically promotes a nostalgia for some supposed bygone golden age. In contrast to these impulses, what is

2. For an account of the "entire history of Jesus Christ," see Jonathan R. Wilson, *God So Loved the World: A Christology for Disciples* (Grand Rapids: Baker, 2001).

called for is a recovery of the practices formed by and witnessing to the grace of God in the life of the church.

Given the essential relationship between the gospel and practice, and given the absence of vibrant, graceful practice in the life of the church today, a recovery of the practices of the church is crucial to continued faithful witness to the gospel.

Many teachers of the church are making significant use of *practice* in their work.[3] Most of the uses that they make of practice will be important to this book. But the account of practice that most significantly shapes this book is that of Alasdair MacIntyre, which we will examine in detail. In MacIntyre's account, practices are part of a social network and receive their meaning from the *telos* toward which they are directed. In other words, practices cannot be isolated from the whole life of a community and the relationships internal and external to it. Nor can practices have meaning apart from the community's conception of the *telos* toward which it is moving.

Since *telos* is an uncommon term but crucial to unfolding the practices of the church, it requires some extended attention. I have taken the word from MacIntyre, who in turn derives his use of it from an understanding of Aristotle. I persist in using the term *telos* rather than some English translation in order to retain the significance it has for Aristotle, MacIntyre, and my account.

Telos is a bit like "purpose" or "goal." It is that toward which something is oriented, toward which it is moving. Or it is that for which something is made, its purpose. But "goal," "purpose," and "orientation" may easily mislead us as translations of *telos*, because in our cultural moment each of those English terms conveys the idea of choice and achievement, whereas *telos*, as used here, is imposed. A hammer cannot choose between sawing boards or driving nails. Its *telos*—driving nails—is given to it by virtue of its identity as a hammer. Of course, depending upon its design, a hammer may have other purposes. The point is that the *telos* of the hammer is given to it, not chosen by it.

---

3. I use "teachers of the church" to refer broadly to all those charged with such responsibility, whether the label is pastor, bishop, Bible scholar, theologian, church historian, homiletician, pastoral counselor, or some other. I also use it to remind us that the first responsibility of such people is to the church, not to the academy.

Likewise, the church does not choose its purpose or achieve its goal; rather, its *telos* is given to it by God, who chooses the church to bear witness to the gospel. The church will do so by demonstrating in its own life the judgment and redemption of God's grace. These claims reflect the argument of Paul's letter to the Ephesians. There Paul writes that he has been given grace "to make everyone see what is the plan of the mystery hidden for ages in God who created all things; so that through the church the wisdom of God in its rich variety might now be made known to the rulers and authorities in the heavenly places. This was in accordance with the eternal purpose that he has carried out in Christ Jesus our Lord" (Eph. 3:9–11).

By God's choice, the life of the church is a witness to God's gracious wisdom. To further that witness, this book attempts to render an account of the life of the church as practices: socially embedded activities that incorporate the church into the *telos* determined for it by God.

To understand this more fully, think again of the celebration of Communion. In most accounts of this activity, the focus is on what happens to the bread and the wine, who may partake, who may administer, and what the act means in relation to salvation. Those are important questions. But here we will take a different approach to ask what the original act of Jesus and his disciples means within the context of Jesus's other social relationships as narrated by the Gospels. We will ask, with whom did Jesus eat, and what do those acts reveal to us about Jesus's socializing? What is the relationship between those occasions and his last supper with his disciples? And what does this act mean for us today as a social practice? How can we better understand and live out its significance as a practice? In the later detailed treatment of "eating and drinking with Jesus" I will also make some concrete suggestions about church practices today.

In everyday life, we use the word *practice* in simple and ordinary ways: piano practice, football practice, choir practice; practice kindness, "practice what you preach"; medical practice, legal practice. The first set regards practice as rehearsal for the real thing; the second set regards practice as acting on a thought or commitment; the third set regards practice as a complex activity encompassing many constituent parts. The way I will use *practice* in this book is

13

closest to the third use, though it also has something of the second in it. My use is furthest from, indeed usually in contrast to, the first use.

The notion of practice has been put to good use in a number of fields today. Later, we will survey those uses. In this section, we will take a close look at the concept of practice that is most determinative for my account, the one developed by MacIntyre in his seminal work *After Virtue*. MacIntyre's argument and his account of practice are so complex that I will introduce them gradually in order to arrive at an understanding that will be the basis for the rest of this book.

In *After Virtue*, MacIntyre analyzes our cultural moment by telling the story of Enlightenment culture. His most telling insight is the claim that in our culture we have abandoned most convictions about the *telos* (the "good," the created purpose) of human life and human activities. This abandonment of *telos* drains our actions of any real meaning and significance. As a result, we cannot give any compelling reason for doing the things that we do, except "What I do makes me feel good" or "I do what I do because this is what I have chosen to do." When we are asked why something makes us "feel good" or why we have "chosen" it, we can do nothing more than repeat our answers.

This present circumstance stands in contrast to the past, when people had a conception of the *telos* of human life and acted in relation to it. In that situation, when asked "Why do you do what you do?" one replied, "Because doing this enables me to achieve the *telos* for which I am made." Of course, not everyone agreed on the *telos*, but most agreed that the proper way to organize human life was in relation to particular convictions about the *telos*. This orientation toward a *telos* gave meaning to a way of life.

Think again of athletes who get up early every morning, follow a strict diet, devote several hours each week to physical exercise. Why? Because they have a goal in mind that can be achieved only by such activities. In the same way, prior to the Enlightenment culture that began in the seventeenth century, people's lives were generally oriented around some *telos*. While athletes understand that certain practices are integral to participating in a specific *telos*, our culture in general has lost this understanding.

After his extensive and profound critique of culture, MacIntyre brings much of his account together in a complicated description of practice as

> any coherent and complex form of socially established cooperative human activity through which goods internal to that form of activity are realized in the course of trying to achieve those standards of excellence which are appropriate to, and partially definitive of, that form of activity, with the result that human powers to achieve excellence, and human conception of the ends and goods involved, are systematically extended.[4]

This definition draws together many aspects of MacIntyre's argument. To understand it, we must unpack each of its elements.

Practices embody a concept of the good. If someone observed your life for a week—the use you make of time, the activities that you engage in, the people you relate to, the settings in which you pursue those relationships, the way you spend your money—what would that observer conclude is important to you? From observing your life, what would that person conclude about your conception of the good? Does your life exhibit practices that reflect or embody your convictions about the purpose or goal of human life? Or is your life a random set of attempts to manage the absence of a *telos* and distract yourself from that absence by entertainment or consumption or addiction?

Now ask that question of the church. Are the activities of the church—of your congregation—oriented toward convictions about the *telos* of the church? If the same observer who watched your life now watched the life of your church for a week or a month, would

---

4. Alasdair MacIntyre, *After Virtue: A Study in Moral Theory*, 2nd ed. (Notre Dame, IN: University of Notre Dame Press, 1984), 187. I read the first edition of this book while pastoring a small Baptist church in Burnaby, British Columbia, and immediately perceived its relevance for my ministry and the life of the church. That perception was later reinforced by my doctoral studies at Duke University. This is now the third book in which I have made use of insights and categories drawn from MacIntyre. For my analysis of MacIntyre, see Jonathan R. Wilson, *Living Faithfully in a Fragmented World: Lessons for the Church from MacIntyre's "After Virtue"* (Valley Forge, PA: Trinity Press International, 1997). For my appropriation of MacIntyre, see Jonathan R. Wilson, *Gospel Virtues: Practicing Faith, Hope, and Love in Uncertain Times* (Downers Grove, IL: InterVarsity Press, 1998).

he or she be able to identify clearly some *telos* around which the church's life is oriented?

Do you have a clear conception of the created purpose of human life that gives meaning and significance to the activities of your life? Do you have a conception of the human *telos* that finds embodiment in practices? Does your church have a clear conception of the human *telos* that is embodied in the life of the church? Do its activities form practices that embody that *telos*? To what does your life and the life of your church bear witness? Practices embody a conception of "the good." What do the practices of your life and your church reveal about your conception of the good?

Practices constitute a community. Practices, by MacIntyre's definition, are not solitary endeavors. They take place within and require a network of relationships. As we engage in practices, a community is formed. I can shoot a basketball at a basket by myself, but I cannot "play basketball"—engage in the practice of basketball—by myself. To engage in a practice requires a whole set of social relationships. Similarly, I cannot engage in Christianity by myself. Even those activities that appear solitary—reading the Bible, praying by myself, and others—depend upon the social network that has preserved and translated the Bible and has developed and passed on the practice of prayer. And beyond that, neither Bible reading nor prayer is faithful unless it is extended into the community.

Practices are oriented to internal goods. This is a difficult concept to grasp, but it is also important. As MacIntyre argues, practices are oriented toward achieving goods that cannot be separated from the *telos* in which they participate. In other words, internal goods are intrinsic to achieving excellence in a particular practice. For example, among those goods internal to excellence in basketball, we might list agility, teamwork, good defense, good rebounding positions, and others. In contrast to these internal goods are external goods. In basketball, we might list as external goods such things as money, fame, and status. While these may be achieved through playing basketball, none is intrinsic to excellence in basketball. One can achieve money, fame, and status by many means other than basketball. Indeed, if one plays basketball in order to achieve one or more of these (external) goods, then one has ceased to engage in basketball as a practice.

This notion of "internal goods" is sufficiently complex and important to deserve extended reflection, especially since so much of our life today is oriented toward external goods. It is certainly possible to engage in a whole range of activities in pursuit of goods that are external to those activities. But to do that makes those activities no longer "practices" in the way I am using the term. Think again of basketball. It is quite possible, in the account that I am giving, to think that a group of friends playing a game of basketball in a community gym on Tuesday evenings are more engaged in basketball *as a practice* than are the elite, multimillionaire basketball players showcased in the NBA.

Practices extend our conception of the good. We must have some conception of the good in order to engage in practices oriented toward a conception of the good. But we never have a full and perfect conception of the good. Rather, our practices enlarge our understanding of the good and our capacities for participating in the good. As one's basketball skills improve, one begins to understand more fully the meaning of teamwork.

Practice in the Church

In the previous section I unpacked MacIntyre's account of practices. That account, though it is the basis for this book, remains within the boundaries of the Aristotelian tradition. For MacIntyre's insights to be helpful to the church, they must be recast according to the Christian tradition. The clearest and most direct way to do that is to reconsider each characteristic of practice in light of the teaching of scripture.

Practices embody a concept of the good. Many passages in the New Testament describe the *telos* of the church in various terms. I will not try to show here that these passages all identify the same *telos* even if they use different terms. Instead, I will briefly consider one of the basic passages, the Great Commission of Matthew 28:19–20: "Go therefore and make disciples of all nations, baptizing them in the name of the Father and of the Son and of the Holy Spirit, and teaching them to obey everything that I have commanded you." This commissioning gives the church its *telos* and makes it clear that certain activities embody that *telos*. The nature of those activities and their relationship to one another will be considered in detail in a later chapter.

In carrying out this commission, the church simply embodies in the new covenant what the people of God were called to in the first covenant. In Deuteronomy 6:6–7, Moses commissions Israel: "Keep these words that I am commanding you today in your heart. Recite them to your children and talk about them when you are at home and when you are away, when you lie down and when you rise." What is this but a "first covenant" description of disciplemaking as the *telos* of the people of God?

Practices constitute a community. The church does not exist apart from the practices that embody its good and constitute it as a community. That is, the church does not have an identity rooted in something other than its practices. There is no identity for the church outside its practices. Its first practice is the discipleship that is initiated and enabled by God's call. Certainly God's call is prior to the church's discipleship, but the constitution of the church is not prior to its own practice of discipleship.

In John's Gospel, Jesus instructs the disciples that their love for one another will demonstrate to the world that they are his disciples. Many of the battles that Paul fought were precisely over which practices would constitute the community of the new covenant—would circumcision? No. For Paul, and eventually for the church, the new covenant required the displacement of some practices, the reorientation of others to a new *telos*, and the learning of some new ones. But what is clear from Romans (esp. 12–14), Galatians, and Ephesians is that Paul's work may be understood in part as the development of practices for the community of the new covenant, Jew and Gentile.

Practices are oriented to internal goods. In Israel's history, we can see clearly certain times when their practices were directed toward external goods. They worshiped, sacrificed, and "honored" the covenant not in pursuit of a relationship with God but in pursuit of a relationship with God for the further (external) purpose of material prosperity, political power, or military security. In the New Testament we can see the same dynamic—Jesus is "followed" in pursuit of some supposed greater good: liberation from Rome, spiritual power, religious status, physical health. But the good of following Jesus is . . . Jesus. As Jonathan Edwards (and John Piper today) reminds us, God's passion is for God's glory. With the psalmist we must confess, "Whom have I in heaven but you? And there is nothing on earth that I desire other than you" (Ps. 73:25).

In the New Testament, the early disciples reflect this mature orientation to the internal good of discipleship. When Peter and John are imprisoned, appear before the court, and are reprimanded and flogged, they leave the court rejoicing not in their ability to heal, not in their evangelistic success, not in their reputation among the people, but that "they were considered worthy to suffer dishonor for the sake of the name" (Acts 5:41). Likewise, Paul reflects this orientation to internal goods in Philippians 1, as he returns several times to the supremacy of Christ, whether he is preaching the gospel or others are preaching, whether others are preaching from sincere motives or not, whether he will die or live. What matters in each instance is the one good—that the gospel of Jesus Christ be made known to those who have not yet heard and believed.

Practices extend our conception of the good. When some fishermen were called as disciples of Jesus of Nazareth, they had some understanding of what that meant; otherwise they could not have begun to follow. But their understanding was certainly incomplete. As they engaged in the practice of discipleship, their understanding of that good and their capacity to participate in it enlarged significantly. Likewise, in the New Testament the call to discipleship is not to do a better job of living out a concept of discipleship that we already have clearly and fully in front of us from the beginning of the Christian life. Rather, in the New Testament (and today) the call to discipleship is to begin an adventure in which we continually grow in our understanding of what it means to be a disciple.

This means that we may begin with an understanding of the sin in our lives that we have to overcome, but we soon discover that our understanding is limited in scope and depth. Or we may begin with an inkling of the sacrifice that is required of us, but we soon discover that we are called to places of service that require greater sacrifice than we first imagined. And we may begin with some slight understanding of the depth of God's love and grace, but that too increases as we practice worship. If we think of some great adventure

19

story—say J. R. R. Tolkien's Lord of the Rings trilogy—we may see there an extended example of this sort of thing. When Tolkien's hobbits and their companions set out, they have only a slight idea of the good toward which they are called. Their understanding and they themselves are profoundly transformed by their practices. In more profound and eternally significant ways, the disciple community's conception of the good is transformed by its practices.

Practices enable us to participate in the good. A change from MacIntyre's language of "achieve the good" to this language of "participate in the good" is crucial to biblical faith. In an Aristotelian tradition, some people are capable of *achieving* the good, if they are male, have the good fortune of being well formed by their parents, and have the leisure to devote to the pursuit of the good. Women, slaves, and those who must labor for a living are incapable of achieving the good.

In the Christian tradition, grace changes all of this. By grace, God makes us participants in the good rather than achievers of the good. This participation in the good, by grace, is available to all—Jew and Gentile, slave and free, male and female. But the contrast is not activity in Aristotle versus passivity in Christ. Rather the contrast is between the activity of achievement and the activity of participation. None can achieve the grace of redemption; anyone may, by God's grace, participate in redemption. This distinction is crucial to understanding the practices of the church, especially in our cultural moment.

In our current place in history in North America, we seem caught between two errors. On the one hand, we confront an extraordinary confidence in the human power to achieve. We see this in our devotion to technology, to cloning, to stem cell therapy, and to all forms of confidence in human powers over nature and the future. For much of society almost everything is possible. On the other hand, we also confront a reaction to this technological arrogance in a flight toward passivity. This passivity is marked by actions intended to dull the anxious belief that almost all human attempts to control nature and the future cause more harm than good. We see the consequences of this loss of confidence in drug use, in dependence upon therapy, and in the enormous resources directed toward entertainment as diversion.

Those same extremes are present in the church when we think, on the one hand, that marketing techniques and management skills will lead to effectiveness, success, and growth. Or when we fall into the error, on the other hand, of thinking that we have no contribution to make, that we are entirely passive.

The correction to these errors is not some synthesis or middle way but a third way of thinking about the church. In this third way, we become participants in God's work by God's grace. This participation embodies precisely the *telos* that Jesus Christ gave to the church, and this embodiment is learned by the church in the practices that we will explore in the coming chapters.

What I have been describing is what Paul also describes in his letters. Paul's description of our lives "in Christ" uses the language of participation. This language of "in Christ" is central to Paul's letter to the Ephesians. Ephesus and the surrounding area was one of the places to be in the ancient world. As home to one of the ancient wonders—the temple of Diana—Ephesus had pride of place. I learned the significance of such pride of place during my fourteen years of living in Santa Barbara, California. On one cross-country trip I found myself chatting with another traveler who had just visited Santa Barbara. As he gushed over its beauty and wealth, I found myself proudly saying, "I *live* in Santa Barbara." As I emphasized "live," I laid claim to the privilege and identity of a Santa Barbaran.

Against the Ephesian pride of place, privilege, and identity, Paul places the believers *in Christ*. This location changes everything about our identity and privilege. The sense of identity and privilege was so great in Santa Barbara that it produced a book, *How to Santa Barbara*, providing a description, only occasionally tongue in cheek, of how a "true Santa Barbaran" was supposed to do things—shop, eat out, drive, travel, and so on. Paul's letter to the Ephesians is extended instruction in "how to *in Christ*." The practices of the church enable us to be in Christ.

Paul's portrayal of our "inheritance" likewise uses the language of activity but not of achievement. Similarly, participation is reflected in the language of inheritance that Peter uses in his first letter and explicitly in the opening chapter of his second letter. Peter knows that our future is certain in Christ and calls us to live now in that reality: "His divine power has given us everything needed for life and godliness, through the knowledge of him who called us by his own glory and goodness. Thus he has given us, through these things, his precious and very great promises, so that through them you may escape from the corruption that is in the world because of lust, and may become participants of the divine nature" (2 Peter 1:3–4). We participate now in the promises and nature of God by engaging in the character formation and practices that Peter calls us to and that we are exploring in this book.

Church as Practice

All of the characteristics of practices that I have described so far may be captured by thinking of the church itself as a practice. Although I would not want us to actually adopt this language as part of our vocabulary, it might help us to think about the church as practice by talking about "churching." Are we churching together? Did we "church" today? The advantage in such language is that it makes us think in new ways about the church, ways that faithfully illuminate the biblical text. The danger in such language is that it denies or at least deemphasizes the institutional character of the church by suggesting that "church" is merely something that "happens" on occasion instead of a continuing embodied presence that persists through history.

Practices cannot be sustained apart from institutional structures. At a minimal level, a basketball team needs to know when and where it is meeting for practice, who the coach is, who has the keys to the gym, who will pump up the balls to the proper pressure, when and where the games will be played, who will play which position, and much more.

Similarly, "churching" requires some institutional form. The question for the church is not how much institution, as if there were some magic threshold for size and complexity of ecclesiastical institutions; nor is it what shape, as if the New Testament enjoined one clear, well-developed organization for the church. Rather, the questions for the institution(s) of the church are whether it is enabling or disabling the practices of the church, whether it embodies the good, whether it serves internal goods, whether it extends our conception of the good, and whether it faithfully participates in the *telos* given by God. The institutions of the church are to serve the practices of the church. That conviction will pervade the following chapters as I seek to describe the activities of the church as practices and thus also render an account of the church as practice.

I look back on my own pastorate with some regret about my failure to recognize the importance of "practicing church." In my first year there, I missed a wonderful opportunity to practice church and to teach the congregation to do so. One of the events by which Edmonds Baptist Church was known in the community was the annual rummage sale. This sale was no small, one-day event. It lasted an entire week and drew people from all over our metropolitan area. The men in the church helped set it up, and the women of the church poured enormous amounts of energy into planning and executing it. I was embarrassed by this event. It did not look like any evangelism program I had studied. And I disliked the fact that it was the only significant source of income for the women's mission circle to dispense through the year. I tried to avoid it, but a phone call from a wise elder in the church shamed me into showing up briefly at the end of the first day.

Now I think of all that could have happened if I had helped to shape this event as a practice of the church. If only I had gathered everyone at the beginning of the first day for a brief reflection on caring for the poor and clothing the naked. If only I had led us in prayers for those who would be working and those who would be shopping. If only I had invited further reflection on how this event was integral to our convictions about the gospel and could be incorporated more fully into our mission. So much could have happened to orient us to our *telos*, form us as a community, give life to internal goods, and extend our conception of the good so that others could hear and believe the good news of Jesus Christ. Today, I write in hope that these chapters may be used by God to enliven a *practicing church*.

2

Worship as Work, Warfare, and Witness

> Question: What is the chief end of man?
> Answer: The chief end of man is to glorify God and
>   enjoy him forever.

This question and answer comes from the Westminster Shorter Catechism, a work from the seventeenth century designed to teach sound doctrine. The answer reflects the clear teleological thinking of an earlier age. What is the created purpose of humankind? To glorify and enjoy God forever. The mission of the church is to display that end, that created purpose, for the entire world to see so that others may come to know their chief end as human beings.

Therefore, the activity of worship—glorifying and enjoying God—is the central practice of the church. Indeed, we must acknowledge in the light of John's vision that worship is the eternal purpose of the church. In the Revelation of John, the vision of worship around the throne builds to a crescendo. First, the four living creatures and the twenty-four elders come in worship:

> You are worthy, our Lord and God,
>   to receive glory and honor and power,
> for you created all things,
>   and by your will they existed and were created. (4:11)

Then after the great drama regarding the scroll, the same actors "sing a new song" to the Lamb:

> You are worthy to take the scroll and to open its seals,
>   for you were slaughtered and by your blood you ransomed
>   for God
>   saints from every tribe and language and people and
>   nation;
>   you have made them to be a kingdom and priests serving our
>   God,
>   and they will reign on earth. (5:9–10)

After this song, the living creatures and elders are joined by the angels:

> Worthy is the Lamb that was slaughtered
>   to receive power and wealth and wisdom and might
>   and honor and glory and blessing! (5:12)

Then in a great crescendo all creatures throughout the cosmos sing:

> To the one seated on the throne and to the Lamb
> be blessing and honor and glory and might
> forever and ever! (5:13)

And all creation worships. If you have ever heard a glorious piece of choral music or tens of thousands singing in praise, then you have heard and seen only a pale imitation of this scene. And even paler is our present knowledge of God's glory and honor and wisdom and might! For those who have truly worshiped and caught, however dimly, a vision of God's majesty, the declaration that we are to glorify and enjoy God forever is cosmic good news.

It is to this activity as a practice that the church is called. It is this practice that most clearly sets the church apart, that most clearly displays our calling and constitutes the church as a community. So I will be devoting three chapters to this central activity of the church.

25

Worship as Work

The practice of worship as work can be easily identified and remembered by reference to *liturgy*. In some churches "liturgy" is the natural and usual way to refer to the activity of worship. Other churches think of themselves as nonliturgical. There is a place for sorting out the differences reflected in these different traditions over planning worship, written prayers and confessions, the participation of the congregation, processionals, vestments, and so on.

But here I refer to *liturgy* for another reason. It is made up of two Greek words that remind us of the work of worship: *laos* = people and *ergy* = work (or energy). So the English word *liturgy* may serve to remind us that worship is the work of the people.

Why is worship the work of the people? First, because worship has to be learned. We don't see this clearly because most of the ways that we learn to worship and learn what to worship are hidden from us. We learn false worship and idol worship as an ordinary part of the human condition. Our society begins very early to shape the ways that we worship and what we worship. Just because we don't have wooden or stone statues in our homes, we think that we are not idolaters. But we are. We organize our lives around affluence, success, comfort, security, health, and entertainment. We worship these idols in the cathedrals of today: shopping malls, gymnasiums, hospitals, cineplexes, auto showrooms, and health spas.

It takes work, strenuous work, to unlearn these habits of false worship and learn to worship the God of Jesus Christ. We must learn to discern the false goods for which we live and the practices by which we pursue them. One of the mistakes we make is thinking that worship of God comes naturally and can be learned "spontaneously," without instruction.

But the Bible is filled with instructions in proper worship. And the history of Israel is filled with their failure to worship properly. It takes work to learn to worship. (This cannot be said too often.) It also takes a people.

Worship is the work of the people because the practice of worship cannot be learned alone. False worship is learned in community, and it must be unlearned in community. And the only way to counter the weight of the community that is constantly teaching us false worship is through the weight of an alternative community. I cannot learn or sustain worship as a practice faithful to the gospel apart from a people who are learning the same. I need others who agree with me on the good in which we seek to participate and the ways in which we may do so. I need others to discern the ways in which I am still worshiping falsely.

Worship is the work of the people. It is restorative not because it is easy but because it reconnects us to the created purpose of humankind. The church is the people who are committed to that project, who expect that to happen when they gather, and who exercise responsibility for its happening.

Since worship is the work of the people, it requires all the gifts that we bring. Worship does not depend upon a narrow range of gifts possessed by a few select people. As the work of the people, it is the work of *all* the people. And planned and written down, or planned and unwritten, or spontaneous and orderly—whatever its form, our worship must liberate and incorporate the whole range of gifts of the people.

If the gifts and talents of all are not involved, then no business, no team, no musical ensemble can truly prosper. We would find it strange to attend a concert in which 90 percent of orchestra members sat in their chairs with their instruments in their laps and never played a note while the other 10 percent carried the workload. How much more strange that description should strike us as a description of the church. Yet it is true of much that we do as the church.

If worship as practice is the work of the people, then we must think carefully about the ways we worship and plan intentionally for our practice of worship to be the work of the people. To do that, we must continually set this claim before the church. No coach of a team simply stands on the sidelines and watches the team practice. Rather, the job of the coach is to point out and correct mistakes, give instruction, demonstrate excellence. Although I think that "coach" is a misleading way to describe the role of pastor, the responsibility of a coach helps us see the importance of instruction in the work of the people.

Moreover, we do not learn a new job merely by imitating someone else. We must also be taught what we are doing and why we are doing it. When I was younger, I was hired to load trucks for United Parcel Service. I received no orientation or training before I began the job and no training on the job. I was terrible at it. I was slow and I made many mistakes. After a few months, I was fired. About two years later, I went back to UPS and asked them to re-hire me—that company paid the best part-time wages in the area. To my surprise, they rehired me. This time I received two shifts of on-the-job training. I discovered that there was a system to loading trucks efficiently and carefully. The challenge of "building a wall" with just the right interlocking of boxes appealed to my delight in patterns and planning. I soon became the trainer for all of the loaders in our "hub." Visiting bigwigs were walked by my truck to see the work that I was doing—all because someone taught me the "practice" of loading a UPS truck.

Worship, of course, is very simple. But it is also very complex because it takes place within the context of our lives. Our lives are set within the context of our relationships with one another, our society, our own histories, and our knowledge of God. These complexities mean that worship is work.

How do we view ourselves in relation to others with whom we gather to worship? Do we understand that we all come in need of God's grace and that no one has any higher standing than another before God? This is clearly the teaching of scripture. While we may have different roles, those roles do not indicate spiritual superiority; they merely represent God's call upon each of us to serve the community as it is constituted by our practice of worship. Paul spends a large portion of 1 Corinthians making this point and turns to it in Ephesians 4.

What has our society taught us to want and to expect? Do we look to worship for entertainment, distraction, illusions? Or do we look for the truth of God that calls us to responsibility, demands our attention, and exposes our illusions? The prophetic condemnation of false worship and call to true worship embody this characteristic of the work of the people.

Are we captive to our own histories when we come to worship? Or do we come ready to do the work of reexamining those histories so that we may become new people? Paul reminds the Corinthians, "This is what some of you used to be" (1 Cor. 6:11), and in Philippians 3 he recounts his history only to celebrate his new identity in Jesus Christ. This transformation of our histories takes place in worship as well as elsewhere.

When we approach worship with intention and reflectiveness as the work of the people, not informally and casually as a "natural" human activity, we unlearn the false goods toward which we are constantly lured and to which we continually fall prey. At the same time, we learn the true good for which we have been made and redeemed in Jesus Christ.

At this point, the practice of worship as the work of the people does not just disentangle us from sin, it also leads us into righteousness by aligning us properly in our relationship to God, to one another, and to all creation. Here the work of the people is not to unlearn but to learn—who God is, who we are before God, and what all creation is before this one God of the universe. But we must be intentional in this and understand that we work to know God so that we may worship more faithfully and truthfully. The failure of God's people in the Old Testament and the New Testament should caution us today to recognize how easy it is to fall into error in our worship of God.

There is no better place to learn these things than the Book of Psalms. In the psalms, we recite and glorify God's character and deeds. We lament the way things are not supposed to be and confess confidence in God's sovereignty. In these psalms, God's people engage in the work of worship. We can learn much today by following the lectionary tradition of reading a psalm each Sunday and being instructed regularly from them in the practice of worship.

Worship as Warfare

The work of unlearning and learning is rooted in conflict between sin and righteousness, folly and wisdom. But I want to extend the notion of conflict one step further to argue that worship is a form of spiritual warfare.

This is dangerous language in a world marked by physical violence that claims religious motivation and justification, not only in

29

international terror but also in domestic terror. However, it is precisely in such times that we must hold on to or recover the biblical teaching on spiritual warfare.

In both testaments, the world in which we live is caught up in the warfare between two kingdoms that are described in a variety of contrasts: sin versus righteousness, death versus life, darkness versus light, Satan versus the Son. This warfare is reflected throughout the Bible and in many aspects of the life of the church. In a passage that addresses these issues most thoroughly, Paul teaches us that "our struggle is not against enemies of blood and flesh, but against the rulers, against the authorities, against the cosmic powers of this present darkness, against the spiritual forces of evil in the heavenly places" (Eph. 6:12). Paul then enumerates the spiritual weapons with which we fight this war: truth, righteousness, peace, faith, salvation, the Spirit and the Word (6:14–17). When we identify enemies in the flesh and use the weapons of this age, we are not engaged in the warfare of the kingdom of God. Kingdom warfare is the warfare not of death and destruction but of good news exemplified in those goods listed by Paul.

When we examine that list, we can see how the practice of worship becomes warfare. In worship we engage in battle with the kingdom of sin. We seek the truth, not lies, about ourselves and God. We are sinners; God is righteous. We come as people with sin; we come before a God who does not tolerate sin. We can come together in God's presence only because God in Christ has made a way. In the same way we celebrate in worship the righteousness, peace, and salvation of Jesus Christ.

We do so in the face of the darkness that wants to claim us and consume us. In Luke's Gospel, the birth of Jesus Christ is announced to the shepherds by an angel. Then the one angel is joined by

a multitude of the heavenly host, praising God and saying,

> "Glory to God in the highest heaven,
>   and on earth peace among those whom he favors."
>   (2:13–14)

The "heavenly host" of this passage is the army of God, come to do spiritual battle with the forces of evil that oppose the birth of the Messiah. They drive back the forces of darkness by worshiping God. When we sing praise to God, declaring the truth about God and ourselves, we too engage in spiritual warfare that drives back the kingdom of sin and participates in that victory already won in Jesus Christ.

In the movie *Romero*, two scenes vividly represent this reality. *Romero* is the story of Father Arnulfo "Oscar" Romero, who was named Catholic archbishop of El Salvador in 1979 as a compromise, a safe appointment in the midst of national turmoil. Romero, however, surprised everyone including himself by becoming the voice of the people against the oppressive wealthy and political powers. In one scene, Romero and many people are driven from a village church by warning gunfire. After Romero quietly leads the people out of the church, he pauses; then with a look that conveys a sudden insight (wonderfully communicated by Raul Julia, who portrays Romero), he leads the people back into the church, gathers the elements scattered by the soldiers, and begins to lead the people in worship—a Catholic mass. In the face of such courage, the soldiers must either retreat or exercise further violence. They retreat.

In another scene, Romero is confronted by a soldier and stripped of his outer garments. A peasant woman runs up to him with a blanket. Romero fixes his gaze on the soldier and says, "Let us pray." Again, the soldiers retreat.

The reaction of the soldiers is not an argument for the utilitarian success of worship. In other cases, worship has been met with great violence, and after Romero's assassination, sixty thousand Salvadorans "disappeared." What these scenes illustrate for us is the call for the church to be faithful to its own *telos*, not some other *telos*. Worship defeats the enemy by keeping the church from being seduced into the *telos* of the enemy.

The war we are engaged in is the struggle not to allow the enemy to determine how we think about God, ourselves, or the rest of creation. The enemy is defeated when we faithfully practice the *telos* for which God has created and redeemed us in Jesus Christ. Thus we participate in Christ's victory and our inheritance when in worship we confess our sin instead of justifying ourselves,

31

when we give thanks to God instead of congratulating ourselves, when we devote our bodily life to praising God in processing, singing, kneeling, raising our hands, and giving instead of devoting our bodily life to the pursuit of sinful counterfeit pleasures and excesses.

Worship as Witness

We are often rightly reminded that the congregation is not the "audience" of worship for which the pastor, musicians, and others "perform." Rather, God is the audience to whom we address our praise. We should not ask whether we liked our worship as if we were consumers whose return business must be earned; we should ask whether God is pleased by our worship. (The criteria of true worship will be explored in the next chapter.) This reminder is a necessary corrective in our age. But it does not tell the whole story, because worship has another audience.

In addition to worshiping before God, the church should be aware that we are worshiping before the watching world. As we engage in the practice of worship and display the *telos* of creation in the redemption of Jesus Christ, we are bearing witness to the good news. For worship to be witness, we simply have to do the work of the people of God. We do not have to twist or skew worship away from its real purpose in order to bend it toward witness.

The work of worship is itself witness, because in worship we are called to declare who God is, who we are before God, and how we are related to the rest of creation. This form of witness may be particularly important at our time and place in history. The church in North America has come to the end of any cultural hegemony that we may have had. Even if we judge that North American culture was never really "Christian," we may nevertheless concur with the judgment that the church held a privileged place in the culture. As that comes to an end, the church's witness to the gospel may often appear to be a plaintive cry for a golden age or pouting in public over lost prestige. In these cases, direct witness to the gospel is difficult to separate from a last grasp at power.

What better way to bear witness to the gospel than to let the world watch a display of the gospel and overhear that good news? Such an approach is not an attempt to manipulate; that is, it is not an even more clever way of sucking people in, like Tom Sawyer pretending to have so much fun painting the fence that Huck insists on painting it himself. The church is not pretending, it is practicing. What the world really needs is what the gospel calls the church to: not more words but more faithful actions. This makes the gospel real, and the words then become lively.

Worship gives concrete reality to the claims of the gospel. Imagine trying to explain the game of baseball to someone who has never seen a game, never seen a baseball field, a pitcher's mound, a leather glove, or a wooden bat. How much work would it take to bring someone to even a minimal understanding of what the game of baseball is all about? Now, imagine explaining baseball to someone while the two of you are standing on a field, walking through a dugout, then sitting in the stands during a game. It still isn't easy, but the words have a life to them, and you can point to the people and events of the game as you explain it.

In the same way, worship makes evident the claims of the gospel. We can point to acts of forgiveness, the work of grace, the exercise of mercy, the expression of discipleship. Just as God's love was demonstrated, made real, enfleshed in Jesus Christ, so today that love is made real in the body of Christ, the church. And worship is the central practice of that life.

This claim that worship is witness before the watching world brings with it the challenge of making worship public. Today, church buildings are less and less "public space." What we need, then, is the creative appropriation of public spaces for the church's worship. Such acts of appropriation take place when congregations worship together in a park, on a wharf, on a university green, in the courthouse square, in the mall atrium, or in the community center. These services must be carefully planned to bear faithful witness to the gospel, but especially when they clearly involve a range of congregations affirming one another's witness to the gospel, they may be a powerful form of witness.

The claim that worship is witness brings a second challenge. To what extent should the worship of the church be shaped by the commitment to witness? To adapt Marva Dawn's phrase, how can we "reach out without dumbing down"?[1] In trying to answer this, we may be caught between two apparently competing emphases in the church today. On the one hand we have the "seeker-sensitive" service that is widely debated. On the other hand we have an emphasis on the "discipline of the secret," which we will consider below.

But these two do not have to be in competition with one another as long as we communicate clearly and speak carefully about them. Seeker-sensitive services are not worship services. They may appear to be so because they often take place on Sunday morning in the space used by a congregation for its worship at other times during the week. But in well-taught and well-led churches these services are expressions of evangelistic outreach that represent a contemporary transformation of a Billy Graham crusade or of an older Youth for Christ rally. The crusade service and the youth rally would not be thought of as "worship services," variations on or replacements for the worship service of a local congregation. In the same way, we should not think of seeker-sensitive services as variations on or replacements for the worship service of the local congregation. Rather, a seeker-sensitive service is a variation on the evangelistic crusade or youth rally. When Paul at Ephesus "entered the synagogue and for three months spoke out boldly, and argued persuasively about the kingdom," or when he "argued daily in the lecture hall of Tyrannus" (Acts 19:8–9), he did so as a seeker-sensitive practice, not as a worship service. So we should not set seeker-sensitive services over against worship as witness, nor should we regard them as two options under one category.

An understanding of worship as witness must also take into account recent commendations of "the discipline of the secret." These commendations draw on the practice of the early church and its retrieval in the work of Dietrich Bonhoeffer to suggest that some of the work of worship, to be done rightly, requires training and preparation.[2] Those who have not been prepared for taking Communion

---

1. Marva J. Dawn, *Reaching Out without Dumbing Down: A Theology of Worship for This Urgent Time* (Grand Rapids: Eerdmans, 1995).

2. For further discussion of this "discipline of the secret," see Jonathan R. Wilson, *Living Faithfully in a Fragmented World: Lessons for the Church from MacIntyre's "After Virtue"* (Valley Forge, PA: Trinity Press International, 1997), 73–76, and references there.

cannot know what it is that they are doing. And if Communion is a time for confessing our sins to one another, extending and receiving forgiveness, and practicing church discipline, then only those who have been properly trained for such practices can participate in them. To have untrained seekers present during such practices would be unfair to them and to the gospel. There are some things that families should take care of in private, not before strangers.

Although I agree with this call to the discipline of the secret and have commended it in my own writings, it is liable to misunderstanding and abuse. It rightly calls for a corrective to our lazy and casual approach to the celebration of Communion and the relative absence of church discipline. These are such serious matters that we should prepare people for them. But this discipline of the secret must not be used to hide from the world the church's own sin, our confession of it, our need to ask for and extend forgiveness, or the necessity of discipline in the church. Like any good practice, the secret discipline may be distorted by false ends and by a quest for external goods. Thus we distort this discipline when we direct it toward some end other than the making of disciples (such as the exercise of power by church leaders) or when we seek some good other than the redemption of Jesus Christ (such as concealing from the world the church's failures).

The Practice of Worship

Worship is the central practice of the church and most fully embraces the teleological reality of our faith. In Western Christianity we are accustomed to thinking of worship as a time when God comes to be present with us. This biblical teaching needs to be enriched by the recovery of another strand of biblical teaching that we encounter in the Revelation of John. There we see that in worship the church is caught up before the throne of God by the Spirit to worship the One who sits on the throne and the Lamb that was slain. In worship we enact who we are in Christ and who we are becoming in the Spirit. This practice requires great effort and intention, it engages us in warfare of the Spirit, and it bears witness to the good news of Jesus Christ as God's grace is lived out in the life of the body of Christ.

35

3

Worship as True, Good, and Beautiful

*I*n the previous chapter, I noted with approval the assertion that we are not to evaluate worship by whether or not we liked it. We are not the audience to be pleased and entertained in worship. Rather, God is the audience who is to be pleased and the world is the audience to whom we bear witness of the gospel.

Those assertions then raise the question, how are we to evaluate our worship? How are we to know when our worship has been pleasing to God and faithful to the gospel? In the previous chapter, I described worship as work, warfare, and witness. But description is not evaluation, and the church can do bad work, lose in warfare, and fail in witness. How are we to know when our work is pleasing and acceptable to God? How are we to know that we are defeating the enemy in worship? How can we tell when our witness is faithful?

In this chapter, I will argue that the criteria by which we are to evaluate worship may be developed under the rubrics of the true, the good, and the beautiful. Before we consider each of these, some preliminary remarks are in order.

These three terms—the true, the good, and the beautiful—do not appear in any biblical passage as the criteria of Christian worship. There is no compelling biblical or theological warrant for their use in this context. Longer lists and other terms may also be useful.

Nevertheless, they provide familiar and comprehensive ways of covering the criteria that scripture uses to evaluate the worship of the people of God.

These terms are familiar from many different settings in the history of ideas. They are the three ideals of Greek philosophy. Immanuel Kant, arguably the most significant philosopher of the Enlightenment, pursues these terms in his three famous critiques: what is true is the subject of his *Critique of Pure Reason*, what is good is the subject of the *Critique of Practical Reason*, and what is beautiful is the subject of the *Critique of Judgment*.

But as we consider these criteria, I will not be concerned with how they have been used in the history of thought. Rather, I will be concerned with how well they serve to represent and summarize the teaching of various passages of scripture on the practice of worship. In the terms that I am using in this book, I will be concerned to bring them into alignment with the *telos* of humankind and all creation revealed in Jesus Christ.

These three criteria are best thought of as three strands of a rope rather than three stages or three pillars. Indeed, to press the image a bit further, we may think of them as three strands of a well-used rope in which the individual fibers have begun to interweave with one another. This image accurately portrays the reality that the true, the good, and the beautiful cannot really be separated from one another. One is not more important than another, except when one is missing and needs special attention for its recovery. Nor is one more foundational than the others, though sometimes particular traditions or congregations may make the mistake of thinking that one is the most important or foundational—usually the one they judge themselves to be particularly successful in meeting. One of the healthiest results that could come from my presentation is the conviction that all three of these criteria must be pursued for worship to be pleasing to God and faithful to the gospel.

These three criteria are roughly equivalent to the standards by which the worship of the people of God was deemed barren by the prophets of the first testament. There, worship was condemned for being idolatrous, immoral, and impure (though I am using the last term in a way slightly different from the Old Testament's). Idolatrous worship is not true worship because it is directed toward a false god. Immoral worship is not good worship because it does not participate in or form us in goodness. Impure worship is not beautiful worship because it falls short of the excellence appropriate to the worship of God. For the prophets, these three failings were no more separable than are the true, the good, and the beautiful. Nevertheless, we can bring each into focus for our edification.

Worship as True

Worship that is true is worship directed toward the one true God. It reflects this conviction—that there is one true God—in its practices. True worship is not a mixture of the worship of several gods, nor is it an uneasy blend of several possible goods. For true worship there is only one God and only one *telos*.

In the Christian tradition we typically contrast true worship to "false" worship. In this chapter, however, I am going to use the term *untrue* rather than *false*. I will do this in order to emphasize the importance of lining up worship positively with our *telos*. Just as a carpenter or a bricklayer will talk about "truing" a wall or a line of bricks, so we may examine whether our worship is true to its *telos*. We can erroneously think that worship goes wrong only when it clearly violates God's will by rebelling against it. But we can also go wrong in our worship by failing to orient worship to its proper end, locate it in the community, and seek internal goods. In short, we make our worship untrue when it is not rightly in line with its God-given *telos*.

True worship requires an understanding of the one true God and increases our understanding of that God. The entire Old Testament is extended training in learning this one true God. Over and over again, the people of God hear declarations of the character and actions of this one true God. Again and again they observe God's character and will in action. And time after time, the people of God get it wrong. Deuteronomy is extended training in the character of Yahweh, the one true God. The Psalms reflect this process in Israel's history. And the prophets provide a concentrated, intense course in learning true worship.

The worship of the people of God becomes untrue when they wrongly construe the God whom they are worshiping and when they try to combine the worship of other gods with the worship of the one true God. The Israelites misconstrue the God whom they are worshiping when they think that ritually and legally correct worship places God under their control. This attempted domestication of God wrongly treats God as something like a petulant giant who has to be mollified. In a reversal of Marx's dictum, this approach is worship as the opiate of the god. As long as we are ritually and legally correct in our worship, God will be drugged and will not notice that God's character and will are being violated in every other area of life. This is the worship that Isaiah condemns in Isaiah 1.

The church commits this same error today when we think that enthusiastic, well-planned, perfectly executed worship excuses affluent, consumptive lifestyles that depend upon unjust economic structures and practices. We also commit this error when we think that beautiful buildings and large offerings will distract God from the tragic, sinful reality that our churches are still some of the most racially segregated institutions in our culture. We fall into this error as well when think that beautiful music and well-crafted sermons make up for our failure to visit those in prison.

These errors lead to worship that is untrue because they are errors in our understanding of God. They reflect the belief that God is not "that than which nothing greater can be conceived" (Anselm's definition in his *Proslogion*) but rather "that than which nothing is more narcissistic." As long as we feed God's narcissism with our worship, we can get away with almost anything. But that is not the character and will of the one true God.

The second way that Israel's worship became untrue was by Israel's attempt to worship other gods alongside Yahweh. The people of Israel sometimes built alternative worship sites—the "high places" regularly denounced in the Books of Kings—and sometimes mixed rituals directed toward other gods in with their worship of Yahweh. In these practices, Israel reveals its unbelief. Unbelief is never simple "unbelief"; it is always unbelief in one or more convictions. The Israelites' mixed worship reveals their unbelief that there is one true God. *After all, the other nations—Assyria, Egypt, Babylon—are having great success. Doesn't that reveal that their gods exist and are equal to and perhaps even exceed Yahweh in power?*

In the very challenging circumstances, the prophets of Israel and Judah come to understand that there *is* only one true God. If Assyria, Egypt, and Babylon are successful, it is because Yahweh, the one true God, has determined to use them to accomplish God's will. The truth about Yahweh is that Yahweh is not the tribal God of Israel but the only God and ruler of the entire cosmos, who requires righteousness and makes the people of Israel witnesses to that truth even in judgment and exile.

Today, the church makes its worship untrue when it mixes the worship of the one true God with the worship of other gods. What this means in particular congregations is best discerned by the gifts within those congregations. However, within this book some questions may be raised for consideration. Does economic or educational status influence who may participate in leading worship? If we belong to a church whose early members died because they refused to confess that Caesar is Lord, should we rethink the presence of our national flag in our places of worship? Would it represent and teach our *telos* better to have the flags of many nations where the church is gathering and the gospel is being proclaimed? Do we sometimes worship the gods of prosperity and material comfort rather than the God of righteousness and suffering servanthood? Has tolerance displaced the costly forgiveness of a holy God in relation to our sin? These and many other questions need to be heard and pondered by a church that seeks to make its worship true to the one God and ruler of the cosmos.

The discipline in the church that guides this true worship is theology. In our present circumstances, theology is often disparaged. In one Christian college that I know very well, for many years the work of theologians was denounced in chapel sermons more often than any other form of work. Certainly some theology should be denounced, and some theologians do not contribute to the faithfulness and witness of the church. That has always been true from Paul's time onward and even extending back into the contest between the true and false prophets of the Old Testament.

But the very denunciation of "theology" is itself a work of theology. If theology is thinking carefully about God's character and will as revealed in Jesus Christ, then the church can never dispense with the work of theology. Our worship is true when our understanding of God is true. Our understanding of God is true only as faithful men and women set themselves to careful preparation for critical, informed reflection on the church's practices.

Therefore the answer to bad theology is not a denunciation of theology and doctrine but the right practice and understanding of the work of theology and the nature of doctrine. When we ask, "Who is this God we are worshiping?" the answer must be the work of theology. The answer itself is Christian doctrine—articulation of what the Bible teaches about God. If we do not have that mature teaching, then our worship remains immature, false worship is uncorrected, and the gospel is lost to our community.

Worship as Good

Although "the good" as a translation of *telos* figures prominently in this book, in this chapter I am using "good" as a reference to morality. The prophets of the first covenant not only condemned the worship of the people of God for idolatry but also condemned it for immorality. The immorality they condemned had two main expressions. One expression of immoral worship is familiar and memorable: the corruption of the worship of Yahweh by acts of cultic prostitution.

Cultic prostitution was widespread in the ancient world; its rituals rival the most pornographic displays of our culture. But the cultic prostitution of the ancient world featured an added element: religious fervor and frenzy. In the term "cultic prostitution," *cultic* is used in a technical sense of *cultus* to refer to the rituals of worship, not in our more typical contemporary meaning of "pertaining to a fringe or marginal religious group." In the ancient world, sexual acts were, as far as we can tell, not the rare practice of fringe religious groups but relatively common elements of worship among central religious groups.

These acts of cultic prostitution were meant to please and stimulate the gods, as the gods were thought to be just like us, only bigger and more powerful. Israel's worship, when it became immoral in

41

this same way, exposed the nation's drift or flight into a false doctrine of God. It is an open question which came first, the Israelites' mistaken belief about God or their lust. Did they begin to think of God as human and then fall into immoral worship to please an all-too-human God? Or were they so stirred by lust and the counterfeit pleasures of sin that they embraced this form of worship and then developed doctrine that supported it? I doubt that we can know. But just as our consideration of "true" worship led us to reflect on the moral consequences of true and false worship, so our consideration of "good" worship should lead us to reflect on the cognitive effect of good and bad worship.

When we engage in morally bad worship, we often reshape our doctrine of God to conform to our error. Think, for example, of the interplay between untrue worship and bad worship in the churches of the German Christian Movement. Many German churches during the rise of the Third Reich worshiped a God of blood and country. This intertwined with the church's complicity in the evil of the Nazis. One may debate which came first, but what is clear is the connection between untrue worship and bad worship that enables and reinforces immorality.

Are we in danger of a similar distortion of worship today? Yes, I believe that we are. When the worship of God becomes significantly intertwined with affirmation of race, nation, or economic status, we have taken a giant step toward untrue and immoral worship. When we tie worship to the protection and prosperity of a race, nation, or class, we have abandoned the internal goods of worship for external goods. From that point, it is a very small step to the loss of good worship. Indeed, that step is often already taken when we abandon the goods internal to worship.

The second way that the worship of the Old Testament people of God became "not good" was by its setting within an unjust society. Because we live in a culture that has separated the private and the public realm, we often think of morality and justice as different categories: morality has to do with our personal, private lives, while justice has to do with our social, public life. With this division, we also often think that worship and Christian discipleship have to do with morality—the personal and private—but not with justice. And when we do develop a concern for justice, we have been so trained not to look to our faith for guidance that we become captive to political and economic programs that have no roots in the biblical tradition.

That division between private and public, morality and justice, is absent from the teaching of scripture and unknown to the faithful people of God. Morality encompasses the issues and areas of life that we so often separate from our faith in a category called "justice." Worship that is good requires a community that seeks justice as intrinsic to its life with God. No amount of worship can compensate for a failure to pursue justice. No worship may be described as true or beautiful unless it also calls God's people to seek justice.

Worship calls us to goodness by making us participants in the grace of God that transforms lives. Worship is not the celebration of a "grace" that has set aside God's concern for justice, but the celebration of God's gracious act of justice in Jesus Christ that makes us righteous and transforms us into the image of Christ. Worship, then, needs to be extended and explicit training given not only in the character and acts of God (worship as true) but also in the character and acts of those who love God (worship as good). In later chapters I will identify some concrete ways that this training may take place.

Worship as Beautiful

There is a superficial reading of the Old Testament that argues that Israel's worship was word centered and image rejecting. This argument is based on a careless application of the command "You shall not make for yourself an idol, whether in the form of anything that is in heaven above, or that is on the earth beneath, or that is in the water under the earth" (Exod. 20:4). Clearly, the people of God are not to represent the one true God with any created thing. However, Israel's worship is far from image rejecting. Later in Exodus 25–31 (seven chapters!), God gives Moses precise and thorough descriptions of the visual elements of Israel's worship. Similarly extensive descriptions take up most of the book of Leviticus and much of Numbers and Deuteronomy. The reason we can casually assert and agree that Israel's worship is word centered and image rejecting is because these are the portions of the Old Testament that we skip over because we find them boring.

The care, precision, and standards of excellence recorded in these passages make it clear that God cares about the beauty of our worship. Indeed, beauty here really represents a call to excellence in our worship of God. But this excellence must be carefully developed from an understanding of worship as a practice that embodies the *telos* of the church, constitutes a community, seeks internal goods, and extends our conception of what beauty means for the church. In a world obsessed with distorted notions of beauty and a church whose members are often wounded by those notions, the church must not deny the importance of beauty but must transform the meaning of beauty by its practice of worship.

In what follows I will use the awkward phrase "not beautiful" where the familiar term *ugly* could be used and may be expected. I adopt this awkwardness for a reason similar to my earlier use of *untrue* instead of *false*. I want to remind us that worship does not have to be recognizably and obviously ugly for it not to be beautiful. Beautiful worship, like true worship, means worship that is shaped by and participates in the *telos* given by God; it does not have to be clearly ugly in order to fall short of beauty, though as we learn more about beautiful worship we may come to see that all worship that falls short is indeed ugly.

Two aspects of the beauty of worship in the Old Testament may instruct us. One aspect is the declaration that the beautiful things that Israel is required to make for its worship are themselves gifts from God through the intelligence, ability, knowledge, and skill with which the "divine spirit" has filled two Israelites, Bezalel and Oholiab (Exod. 31:1–11). Moreover, all Israel participates in this making through their gifts. In Exodus 25 the gifts of the people of God become the material from which beautiful worship is crafted by those specially called to such work. So the beauty of Israel's worship depends upon the giftedness of specific people, but it also draws on the gifts of the many.

This is an important guide to our practice of worship as we identify those who are skilled in beauty and at the same time incorporate the gifts of all. We do not have to choose between "the professionals" and "the amateurs." We worship as one body with many gifts.

There does not have to be a compromise between excellence and widespread participation.

In the church, then, many give money for the support of and use by those who will provide music, images, drama, sermons, and other elements of worship that are beautiful. One may bring a story that is read or performed by another. One person may design a classroom that is built by another. Together, these various gifts participate in our *telos* as the people of God, form a community, teach and extend our understanding of the good to which we are called.

Another aspect of the beauty of worship in the Old Testament is the regulations for ritual purity. During Old Testament times, many different actions and conditions made one "impure," that is, prohibited from joining the congregation in the temple for the worship of God. Sometimes these conditions, such as being a eunuch, were permanent and thus permanently excluded one from worship. Other conditions, such as touching a dead animal, were temporary and required a ritual of purification before one could be readmitted to worship.

By the time of Isaiah 56, however, the prophet was foreseeing a time when the purity laws would no longer pertain, when eunuchs and foreigners would have a place of honor within God's house and God's family (Isa. 56:1–8). This transformation does not signal an abandonment of beauty or excellence in worship; rather, it signals an extension of Israel's understanding of the *telos* of the people of God. The beauty of worship, Israel now understands, is God's rule over the entire cosmos and the redemption of people from every tribe, tongue, and nation.

The worship of the people of God in the Old Testament became "not beautiful" when they misconstrued the character of God. One of the ways this misconstrual became evident was their offering of substandard sacrifices. God required that the best of the flock, without spot or blemish, be sacrificed to him. This requirement should have taught the Israelites to love God alone and to look to God for their lives. But they often turned from this requirement, offering God something less than the best because the best would bring them the highest price at the market or the tastiest meal at home.

The other way that the Israelite people misconstrued the character of God was hoarding God's blessing for themselves. God's intention in calling Abraham and blessing Israel was that they be a blessing to others—a light to the nations, showing them the way of the one true God. But the people of Israel mistook God's blessing for their right and privilege. Instead of the blessings becoming resources for mission, the blessings became sources of oppression. Instead of gifts that flowed through them to others, they became possessions to be protected.

The church falls into these same "not beautiful" errors. When we fail to give to God first in our gifts and time, we are giving God substandard worship even if the spots and blemishes are not so obvious. One of the most pervasive ways we fail the test of beauty today is when we are not rested and relaxed for worship. Our schedule and lifestyle can be so hectic that by the usual time of worship, Sunday morning, all we can do is stay awake. We have little energy, and we are distracted by the morning news, the sales flyers, lunch plans, or anticipation of the big game on TV. Each of these is a regular feature of our worship, and each is as much an abomination to God as was a substandard sacrifice under the first covenant. We are to bring God our best. And just as the offering of the best of the flock was an economic issue for Israel, so today we face economic questions in our giving as a part of practicing church. (I will discuss this more extensively in a later chapter.)

Another way that our worship is "not beautiful" is our failure to reflect the work of God among all peoples. Our one-color, one-culture, one-class churches are ugly to God. They do not embody the *telos* of creation and redemption in Jesus Christ. They do not embody the practices of that *telos*—the redemption of people from every tribe, tongue, and nation. If anything today reflects the mercy and patience of God, it is God's willingness to give the church time to repent. But God's patience does not last forever and the time of judgment is already at hand.

The beauty of the gospel, its attractiveness and persuasiveness, is in part the glorious reality that in Jesus Christ "there is no longer Jew or Greek, there is no longer slave or free, there is no longer male and female" (Gal. 3:28). The ugliness of the church is that very little of our practice bears witness to this beautiful, heartrending truth. God have mercy on us. God transform us by your grace. (By the way, if you are moved by the previous paragraphs, here's a piece of advice I give friends who bemoan the church's lack of racial and class diversity: find a congregation in which the majority are different from you, then join it. When you join, the congregation will immediately become more diverse.)

Worship That Is True, Good, and Beautiful

This chapter has been short on specific examples of true, good, and beautiful worship. I have given some biblical and historical examples. And I have identified some of the ways that these criteria may be violated. But these criteria really are just that: criteria to be used in a communal process of discernment. Today, worship is one of the divisive focal points in the life of many congregations. Congregations often find themselves in the midst of disagreement and division without knowing quite how they got there and how to reconcile. Other times congregations find themselves deeply at odds over preferences that seem to result in nothing more than power struggles. In this instance, no matter who "wins," everyone loses.

These criteria for the practice of worship can do a lot to disentangle disagreement and reconcile worshipers. These criteria provide a means of carrying on a process of discernment and even locating an argument about worship so as to take people beyond personal preference and power struggles with one another. These criteria, approached properly, can help people identify common aims: that worship be true, good, and beautiful. Their disagreements may then become part of a process by which they discern together how to enter into the practice of worship to participate in the *telos* given by God. This observation does not eradicate disagreement, misunderstanding, or conflict. But it does locate such things in their proper relationship to the practices of the church. Moreover, it makes possible continuing witness to the gospel and growing understanding of the gospel even as a congregation struggles to discern its way to practicing worship.

In a less conflicted situation, these criteria may also aid a congregation, its leaders, and its pastor(s) in evaluating the worship life of the church. We may ask, for example: Which of these criteria seems most important in a particular congregation or tradition? Have we achieved a proper balance between these in our worship? When we look at the life of our congregation, do we see symptoms of the neglect of one or more of these criteria? Do we see symptoms of an overemphasis on one or another? Such questions make use of these criteria to identify, maintain, and restore the healthy worship of the church.

These criteria for worship neatly and positively summarize the biblical injunctions against idolatry, immorality, and impurity. As we practice church in the activity of worship, we must be constantly concerned with the truth, goodness, and beauty of our worship. These criteria force us to set aside our own taste and temperament so that we have to engage in worship in relation to God's work of creation and redemption in Jesus Christ. The question for worship is not *Did I like it?* but, *Is it true to God's character and will? Does it transform us by God's grace? Is God getting our best?*

These questions force us to continually return to the elements of practice in order to discern the quality of our worship, the places of weakness and failure, the places of neglect and distortion, and the places of faithfulness to and participation in God's work.

4

Worship as Trinitarian Practice

We Christians spend more time together worshiping than in any other activity. Certainly we do many other things: Bible study, evangelism, fellowship, committee meetings. But the thing we do *together* more than any other is worship. Yet we seldom give sustained, explicit, *theological* attention to our worship. We may argue about the appropriateness of musical style, we certainly argue about the order of worship, we still roast the preacher for Sunday dinner—or the chaplain over coffee and doughnuts—but even these arguments are usually couched in sociological or political language. We have lost the ability to think and argue theologically about Christian worship; we desperately need to recover that ability.

At one level, a recovery is going on as a number of significant theologians are leading the way to a rediscovery of the centrality of the practice of worship for theology. They argue persuasively that theology must recover a sense of its connection to the practices of the church—that theology is primarily reflection on the practices of the church, not on the practices of the university. In previous chapters I have given an account of worship as a practice. In this chapter, I add to that account by seeking to reflect theologically on our practice of worship.

In the context of the argument of this book, I mean for this chapter to accomplish two purposes. First, I want to continue to

49

advance an account of worship as the foundational practice of the church. This much should already be clear. But I want, second, to demonstrate the significance of the doctrinal heritage of the church for the practices of the church. Too often we have allowed a debilitating distinction between practitioners and theoreticians in the church. While this distinction is defensible and helpful for distinguishing gifts, callings, and circumstances, it becomes debilitating when we allow the two types of workers to ignore one another. Theoreticians converse only with one another, and practitioners do the same, to the detriment of the church, which needs these two in conversation with one another. This entire book is, in part, an attempt to overcome this distinction. In this chapter, I draw on the doctrinal tradition of the church that belongs to my calling as a theologian in order to guide reflection on a practice of the church.[1]

Of course, there are many doctrines from which we could reflect theologically on worship. For example, on the basis of a theological anthropology, one could argue that worship must concern the whole person. Or, focusing on the central event of Christian faith, one could argue that the form of worship should reflect the life, death, and resurrection of Jesus Christ so that sinners who believe in Christ may be reconciled to a holy God.

Here I will consider our practice of worship from the perspective of the doctrine of the Trinity. Many of us think of the Trinity as a rather mysterious doctrine that we simply affirm without much understanding. As I will later argue, trinitarian faith certainly involves mystery. But the trinitarian conviction of the church also serves as the safeguard and the foundation of the meaning of what Jesus Christ accomplished. Thus, trinitarian doctrine and christological doctrine are intrinsically related.

If we can avoid trivializing the majestic (and unfortunately overfamiliar) John 3:16, we can see this:

> For God so loved the world that he gave his only Son, so that everyone who believes in him may not perish but may have eternal life.

1. For another contribution to this project of overcoming this disconnect between doctrine and practice, see the appendix, where I critique some practitioners' accounts of the church.

In terms of later reflection, the "God" of this verse is the Father. But the church recognizes that the New Testament does not allow us to separate the Son from "God" in any substantial way. The Son is also God—incarnate. And the New Testament teaches us that belief in the Son is the work of the Spirit. Indeed, John 3 begins with Jesus's claim that we must be born of the Spirit. So working for our salvation we have the Father, who sent the Son; the Son, who gives and is given for our forgiveness; and the Spirit, who births us into the kingdom of forgiveness and life. There are three, Father, Son, and Holy Spirit; yet there is one God. This threeness and oneness is the Christian doctrine of the Trinity that guides our thought about God and God's relationship to humanity.[2]

If the Trinity is, in part, the rule for how we think about God's own life and about God's relationship to us, then all of our worship of God should be ruled by this doctrine. I invite you to reflect with me on the trinitarian form of Christian worship.

Before considering the oneness and threeness of the Trinity as rules for our worship, I must make four general comments. First, the doctrine of the Trinity is more than a "rule" for how we worship, though that is how we will consider it here.[3] Second, in what follows I will draw on the "Western" and "Eastern" doctrines of the Trinity. The Western tradition is the familiar heritage of most of us, but both of these traditions are within the boundaries of Christian orthodoxy and contribute to our understanding of Christian worship. Third, my remarks in this chapter are attempts to find a place to begin our consideration of worship with the right questions, not end our conversation with clear-cut, definitive pronouncements. Fourth, my own worship takes place within the context of the free church tradition. Therefore, my comments may apply more directly to that tradition than other traditions, though I hope to illuminate the practice of worship in all Christian communities.

2. For a guide to historical and contemporary reflection on the doctrine of the Trinity as well as a helpful bibliography, see Roger E. Olson and Christopher A. Hall, *The Trinity* (Grand Rapids: Eerdmans, 2002).

3. George A. Lindbeck argues for the notion of doctrines as rules in his influential book *The Nature of Doctrine: Religion and Theology in a Postliberal Age* (Philadelphia: Westminster Press, 1984). Although I believe the notion is useful and apply it in this chapter, I disagree with some aspects of Lindbeck's argument.

Oneness

The oneness of God as Trinity is the emphasis carried by the Western tradition. Now the West certainly affirmed the threeness of God and remained within the boundaries of orthodox doctrine. But in their concern to avoid tritheism and affirm monotheism, Western theologians began with God's oneness and chose language that safeguarded that oneness.

Augustine was the great trinitarian theologian of the West.[4] His psychological analogy for the Trinity dominated the church's thought for many centuries, and his choice of language for the oneness and threeness of God placed the emphasis on God's oneness. As his analogy for God's oneness and threeness, Augustine used the human person, who, though one, also has threeness: memory, understanding, and will. But this analogy, which Augustine used in various ways (De Trinitate 8–10), clearly emphasizes the oneness of God. And in his struggle to translate the Greek terms of the creeds into Latin, Augustine chose words that emphasize God's oneness.

This emphasis on God's oneness reminds us that we must not divide God's being or God's character. God is not divided against Godself. We must not, for example, contrast the Father's wrath to the Son's mercy and the Spirit's gentleness. Father, Son, and Spirit are equally wrathful toward sin, merciful toward the sinner, and gentle with all.

This "rule of oneness" has important implications for worship. We are often tempted to think of worship as more fitting to one or another of the three "persons" of the Trinity. Thus, majestic, processional, traditional worship is said to reflect a preference for the Father. Informal, friendly worship is said to reflect a preference for the Son. And emotional, celebrative worship reflects a preference for the Spirit. But if we apply the rule of oneness, then we can see that we are wrong to think that we can divide God against Godself in our worship preferences. If God is majestic, then we (in the strongest language) lie about the Son's divinity if we think of him exclusively as the "friendly" person of the Trinity. If the Father befriends us through Christ's work, then we lie about the Father's

---

4. See Augustine's De Trinitate, published in many editions.

divinity when we portray him as the remote, aloof person of the Trinity. God is one in majesty, friendship, and passion. This is one place where we must start to think theologically about the trinitarian form of our worship.

Another aspect of the emphasis on the oneness of God has to do with God's work. In the Western tradition, theologians developed the notion of "appropriating" the work of God to one of the persons of the Trinity. Thus, the "appropriate" work of the Father is creation, the "appropriate" work of the Son is redemption, and the "appropriate" work of the Spirit is sanctification. But in the tradition this notion of appropriation was safeguarded by the prior emphasis on the oneness of God. So even though the appropriate work of the Father is creation, the church recognized that the Son and the Spirit are also involved in creating. The same is true of redemption and sanctification: Father, Son, and Holy Spirit are all at work in these ways. Thus, although we may speak of an economy in God's work, we may not divide the work among the persons. It is the one God who creates, redeems, and sanctifies.

This understanding of the rule of oneness has two implications for worship. First, for communities that are wrestling with the possibility of changing trinitarian language in their worship practices from Father, Son, and Holy Spirit to Creator, Redeemer, Sanctifier, this rule prohibits such a change of language since that change limits to one person that which is the work of the triune God. Second, in communities that are committed to the language of Father, Son, and Holy Spirit in their worship, we must recognize that language about creation, redemption, and sanctification may seem to us primarily language respectively about the Father, Son, and Spirit. But we must go beyond that to recognize, for example, that language about God's work of sanctification includes the Father and the Son as well as the Spirit. When we praise God for God's work of sanctification, we are not merely worshiping the Spirit; we are worshiping the one God who is Spirit, Son, and Father.

In this section on the oneness of the Trinity as a rule for worship, we have looked at issues that are sometimes thought of in terms of "styles" of worship. That kind of thinking, however, conceals the more profound theological questions that I have raised here. These questions are only a place for us to begin our consideration of worship; they are not a prescription for how to worship. But I am convinced that we must begin thinking about worship at this level in order to keep our worship true.

Threeness

The threeness of God as Trinity is the emphasis carried by the Eastern Christian tradition. Although the Eastern Christian tradition is unfamiliar to many of us, it is an ancient, orthodox expression of Christian faith. Much as the Western tradition affirms the threeness of God, while emphasizing God's oneness, and remains within the boundaries of orthodox Christian doctrine, so also the Eastern tradition affirms the oneness of God, while emphasizing God's threeness, and remains within the boundaries of orthodoxy.

For many centuries this most ancient theological tradition was carried by the variegated Orthodox communion, which for theological, cultural, and political reasons was isolated from the Western tradition (and vice versa). Recently, however, the work of Orthodox theologians has become more accessible to the West, and theologians in Western traditions have found significant resources for their own theological thinking in the Orthodox tradition.[5]

Indeed, there are a number of celebrated cases in which evangelicals have joined the Orthodox communion. I do not feel such an attraction, nor is this chapter an advocacy of such a move. Nevertheless, like many others, I do find significant resources in the Eastern Christian tradition that open up the meaning of our faith in new ways.

In its doctrine of the Trinity, Eastern Orthodoxy begins with the threeness of God. John of Damascus is the most important Eastern Orthodox theologian, but he does not play the dominant role in the East that Augustine plays in the West. Although there is not

---

5. Among the Orthodox theologians in the West are Alexander Schmemann, John Meyendorff, and Vladimir Lossky. The recent translations of Sergius Bulgakov's work makes the thought of this great Russian Orthodox theologian available in the West. Western theologians who have been influenced in different ways by Eastern Orthodoxy include Geoffrey Wainwright, Jürgen Moltmann, Robert Webber, and Cornelius Plantinga Jr. A helpful introduction to Orthodox Christianity for North American Christians is Anthony Ugolnik, *The Illuminating Icon* (Grand Rapids: Eerdmans, 1989).

one dominant theologian of the Trinity to whom we may point in the East, in that tradition the language used for the Trinity clearly seeks to emphasize God's threeness.

The analogy used in the East particularly reflects this threeness. The Eastern view is often called the social Trinity because Eastern Orthodox theology uses a social analogy for the Trinity: God as family. Thus, the emphasis in the East is on the dynamic nature of God's life. In God's threeness, God is related to Godself. The Father, Son, and Holy Spirit enjoy a dynamic life together, glorifying and loving one another. The threeness of God reminds us not to think of God as static or as an individual. Rather, we must think of God as eternal, dynamic fellowship.

This rule of threeness has important implications for our worship. First, this rule leads us to think of worship as something that happens not merely before God but within God's own life. Worship is not merely something we present to God; it is our participation in the life of God, in the fellowship of the threeness of God.

Now this language sounds strange to our Western ears, so let us take note of some of the biblical language with which it agrees. In the New Testament we are told that the Father loves and glorifies the Son; that the Son glorifies and obeys the Father; that the Spirit glorifies the Son and reminds us of what the Son taught; that the Son teaches only what he learns from the Father. When we focus our attention on one person of the Trinity, our gaze is immediately directed to another person. We look upon the Father and are told to look at his beloved Son; we look to the Son and he says wait for the Holy Spirit; we look to the Holy Spirit and see Jesus glorified; we look to Jesus and he directs us to the Father's glory. And on it goes, leading some theologians to talk of the holy dance of the Trinity, each loving and glorifying the other.

When we look for the language of the Christian life, we also find in the New Testament language reflected in Eastern Orthodoxy. Not only are we taught that Christ is in us, but we are also taught that we are in Christ. To be "in Christ" is to *participate* in his life, that is, eternal life, which is the character of God's life that is made possible by Christ. Thus, to be in Christ is to participate in God's life. To be "in the Spirit" is again the language of sharing in God's own life. So we see that the language of Eastern Orthodoxy, though unfamiliar to us, is rooted in the language and imagery of the New Testament.

In this understanding, as I have said, worship is not merely something we do outside of God. Rather, it is our participation in the life of the Trinity. This deepens and extends our understanding of the *telos* of worship and of the goods internal to its practice. This participation makes worship more solemn, grave, and holy and, at the same time, more celebrative, free, and loving.

Following closely on this point is another implication of the rule of threeness. If the dynamic life of the threeness of God is kept in view, then we are led to think of worship not as mere human work but as the work of humanity enabled by God.

In many contexts, it is helpful to be reminded that in worship we are wrong to think that the congregation is the audience while the pastor, musicians, and others are the worshipers, or worse, the performers, and God is relegated, at best, to the role of observer. In place of this faulty picture, we are told that the people in the congregation are the worshipers, the pastor, musicians, and others lead or enable worship, and God is the audience.

This is a very important step in the right direction. But following the rule of threeness, we must go one step further: God is the enabler of our worship. That is, just as creation, redemption, and sanctification have an economy within the threeness of God, where we may speak of each person's having a role to play without threatening the oneness of God, so in worship we may speak of the economy of God.

In speaking of the economy of God in worship, we must speak boldly of God's threeness. In God's economy of worship, the love that God extends to us in redemption is returned to God. The love that comes to us from the Father, through the Son, by the Holy Spirit, is returned by the Holy Spirit, through the Son, to the Father. Thus, in worship God is not simply present to us as audience and judge; God is also present with us, glorifying God's own self and perfecting our worship through the enabling of the Spirit, the mediation of the Son, and the sending of the Father.

Some might be tempted to distort this understanding into an excuse either for shoddiness in worship or for unfaithfulness in living—we have no work to do because God does the work for us.

But rightly understood, the claim that God is with us in worship calls us to ever higher passion for excellence and faithfulness: Holy, Holy, Holy, Lord God Almighty, Father, Son, and Holy Spirit, as we worship in you. This is the practice of worship that participates in the *telos*, forms the worshiping community, and realizes the goods internal to right practice.

A Trinitarian Practice of Worship

To confess God as triune is, among other things, to commit ourselves to thinking about our faith and practice according to certain rules. In this chapter I have sought to find some ways to begin thinking about our worship in trinitarian terms. But ultimately, to confess God as Trinity is to confess the mystery of God who redeems us in Jesus Christ. Before this mystery, all of our words fall short of God's glory.

We must end our thinking about God as Trinity as Augustine ended his great treatise on the Trinity: with the confession, first, that we cannot but think and talk about God, because God has redeemed us in Jesus Christ, and, second, that we always fall short and stand in need of God's forgiveness: "O Lord, one God, God the Trinity, whatsoever I have said in these books that comes of thy prompting, may thy people acknowledge it: for what I have said that comes only of myself, I ask of thee and of thy people pardon" (*De Trinitate* 51).

We stumble to think rightly about God, but with Paul all of our thinking about the God who redeems us in Christ ends, not in further talk about God, but in worship of God—in doxology:

> O the depth of the riches and wisdom and knowledge of God! How unsearchable are his judgments and how inscrutable his ways!
> "For who has known the mind of the Lord?
>   Or who has been his counselor?"
> "Or who has given a gift to him,
>   to receive a gift in return?"
> For from him and through him and to him are all things. To him be the glory forever. Amen. (Rom. 11:33–36)

This confession is indeed an exemplary expression of worship according to a trinitarian rule. To confess God as triune is inherently to worship God, who gathers us to the end for which we are made so that we live. In bringing us to life, God breathes into us the Spirit who directs our practice of worship through Christ to the Father.

5

Worship as Language School

*I*f worship is to be a trinitarian practice that is good, true, and beautiful and engages the people of God in work, warfare, and witness, then it must be grounded in and guided by the deepest convictions of the church, not the lies of the world. For that to be so, the life of the church must be intentionally theological. And theology must be intentionally responsible to the church, not the academy. The place where theology and the life of the church come together most fully is worship. It is there that the language of theology is learned in practice, and it is there that the practice of the church is scrutinized by theology.

In this chapter I will eventually turn to worship as the foundational practice of the church. But before I get there I will first add more theology to the account that I am giving and also locate one aspect of the work of the pastor within the "practicing church." After laying a theological foundation, I will suggest that we think of pastors in their many activities as *language teachers* who enable the people of God to appropriately speak and practice the language of faith in Jesus Christ.[1]

---

1. An earlier version of this chapter was published as Jonathan R. Wilson, "The Pastor as Language Teacher," *Crux* 31 (June 1995): 15–22, a special issue of *Crux* in honor of the ministry of Roy Bell. The idea for that original essay came to me while I was pastor of Edmonds Baptist Church, reading George A. Lindbeck, *The Nature of Doctrine: Religion*

Sometimes, by looking at a familiar object in a new light or from a different angle, we may see things that we have never seen before, even though they have always been there. That is what I hope to accomplish in this chapter—to look in a new way at the life of the people of God and some of the familiar activities of pastors.

I will develop my account first by referring to some works that have guided my thinking about the pastor as language teacher. After I have established the basic idea of the pastor as language teacher, I will give some examples of what this would look like in practice. Based on this exploration, I will consider why we need pastors, why pastors are not all we need, and how worship is central to our learning the language of faith in Jesus Christ.

Sources

In an earlier chapter I introduced the work of Alasdair MacIntyre as a contribution to thinking carefully about the practicing church. Here I will introduce the work of two theologians to thicken our understanding of the practicing church. This approach gives the chapter a bit of a different feel from the previous three, but eventually I will bring this work back to the practice of worship. In this chapter, I am seeking to extend theologically our understanding of practices.

One of the most influential and discussed books in recent theology is *The Nature of Doctrine*. In that book, George Lindbeck argues for a cultural-linguistic understanding of religion over against cognitive-propositionalist and experiential-expressivist understandings.[2] In a cultural-linguistic understanding, religion is the life and language of the community of faith. In a cognitive-propositionalist understanding, religion is the belief system of the community of faith about "objective realities." In an experiential-expressivist understanding, religion expresses the experience of people in spiritually symbolic terms.

Since I do not intend to write about Lindbeck's work but rather to make use of it, the important point here is that his cultural-linguistic

---

and Theology in a Postliberal Age (Philadelphia: Westminster Press, 1984), and taking Roy's class in pastoral care at Carey Theological College.

2. Although Lindbeck's typology is arguably applicable to all "religions," I will refer it to Christianity, as he, for the most part, also does.

approach locates theology firmly within the community of faith, as an expression of and guide for its life and witness. In Lindbeck's proposal, doctrines regulate the life and witness of the people of God. The meaning of a doctrine is found in the use the community makes of the doctrine: "Thus for a Christian, 'God is Three and One,' or 'Christ is Lord' are true only as parts of a total pattern of thinking, speaking, feeling, and acting. They are false when their use in any given instance is inconsistent with what the pattern as a whole affirms of God's being and will" (64). Since doctrines rule our life together, they interpret our experience, rather than our experience interpreting our doctrine. So, for example, "the cross is not to be viewed as a figurative representation of suffering nor the messianic kingdom as a symbol for hope in the future; rather, suffering should be cruciform and hopes for the future messianic" (118).

In Lindbeck's view, then, theology serves the community of faith by helping us to use the language of our convictions to shape our life and witness so that we are faithful to what God is doing in Jesus Christ and so that our witness is intelligible and applicable to our world.

Before Lindbeck, I encountered the importance of language for understanding the task of theology through the work of Paul Holmer. In *The Grammar of Faith*, Holmer presents (among many others) three arguments about theology and language that are central to an account of the pastor's role as language teacher.[3] First, Holmer argues that learning theology is like learning a language. More specifically, theology is the grammar of faith. Therefore, we learn theology the way we learn language. We may initially learn the grammatical rules of a language by memorization, but at some point we are no longer conscious of the rules, we simply speak the language. Others may learn a language by immersing themselves in it and mastering it. But we still need the grammar of the language, so that we begin to understand how it works and how it may go wrong.

If this is the case, learning theology is not an end in itself. It is, rather, a means to learning the language of faith and of becoming more faithful. Holmer's account makes living central to Christianity, but it does not devalue theology or dispense with it. Rather, Holmer gives us an account of the proper place and function of theology. So

3. Paul L. Holmer, *The Grammar of Faith* (New York: Harper and Row, 1978).

theology must find its place in relation to the practices of the church and as one of those practices.

Second, the language of theology is the language *of* faith, not language *about* faith. Just as we learn French not by learning about French but by actually learning French—its vocabulary and grammar—so also we learn theology not by learning about faith but by becoming faithful.[4] Theology, then, is not a "free creation." It is determined by God's prior work that culminates in Jesus Christ (4). When we confuse the task of theology and think that it is *about* faith rather than *of* faith, it appears "that theology is painfully abstract, that it is a specialist's domain, that it is impractical, that it is of no use to the laity, and that it is about matters that do not and cannot concern those who are nonacademic" (1). But when we practice theology as the language of faith, then theology takes its rightful place within the disciple community.

Third, Holmer draws on the work of Ludwig Wittgenstein, a twentieth-century Austrian philosopher who taught at Cambridge, in order to argue that words do not refer; rather, people refer by using words (92). This means that "the whole business of using theology as grammar requires also that we refer our nation, our world, our selves, our future, to God" (26). It also means that the liveliness of a language depends largely upon the lives of those who use it. Thus, "personality qualifications become exceedingly important for this kind of learning and thinking" (68). That is, the vividness of the language of faith is, in large part, dependent on the vividness of the lives of the faithful.

So in spite of differences that do not concern us here, Lindbeck and Holmer provide us with some directions for thinking about theology in the context of a cultural and linguistic system that is the life of the church. My concern here is not to present direct arguments for Lindbeck's and Holmer's views. They and others have pretty well exhausted the arguments for and against, and possible modifications of, their views.[5] Instead, I want to make use of their proposals in order

4. I am reminded of the quip that Americans study foreign languages, others learn them.

5. For sympathetic responses to Lindbeck by evangelicals, see Clark H. Pinnock, *Tracking the Maze* (San Francisco: Harper and Row, 1990), and Stanley J. Grenz, *Revisioning Evangelical Theology* (Downers Grove, IL: InterVarsity Press, 1993). For a more critical appraisal, see

to illuminate the life of the people of God and the work of pastors as a part of that life. In so doing, I am seeking to be faithful to their understanding of theology.

On the basis of Lindbeck's and Holmer's insights we may begin to understand the pastor as language teacher. First, we may think of the pastor as a grammarian of the faith for a congregation. That is, one of the responsibilities of a pastor is to teach the grammar of the faith. In the context of an understanding of the church as a community shaped by its practices and its language, the pastor is responsible for teaching and guarding the grammar of the faith. The most direct fulfillment of this responsibility is in catechism or discipleship classes. In these settings the pastor teaches others the basic grammar of faith in Jesus Christ—the Trinity, Christology, salvation by grace, and others. Other times for teaching this grammar may arise in sermons, in committee meetings, in counseling, and in casual conversation.[6]

The pastor, however, is more than a grammarian; the pastor is also a language teacher. As Holmer notes, being able to speak a language is more than knowing the grammar. One must be able to use grammatical knowledge in order to speak the language and put it to work in appropriate ways. So the pastor must not simply teach the grammar of the faith, he or she must also teach others how to use that language. Here the pastor's calling is to refer all of life to God revealed in Jesus Christ. The pastor must put the language of the faith to work, teaching others how to refer their work, their family, their feelings, and their fears to the gospel.

This latter responsibility constitutes the majority of the pastor's work as language teacher. In sermons, in counseling, in business meetings, the pastor is called to speak faithfully. So the sermon becomes an occasion when the pastor teaches the Christian way of speaking about whatever issue is at hand. Scripture becomes our textbook; the pastor's time in exegesis is time learning the language of the faith; the sermon then extends that language into the lives of the hearers. The focus of the sermon is not so much on interpreting the text as it is

---

Alister McGrath, *The Genesis of Doctrine* (Oxford: Blackwell, 1990). See also a wide-ranging symposium, Bruce D. Marshall, ed., *Theology and Dialogue: Essays in Conversation with George Lindbeck* (Notre Dame, IN: University of Notre Dame Press, 1990).

6. In the next part of this chapter I will further develop this assertion by giving some specific examples.

on interpreting the world according to the text. The sermon makes the gospel relevant to our lives, not by translating it into terms and concepts already accepted but by extending its language over the whole of our lives.

In counseling, the pastor listens to others speak about their lives and seeks to help them speak more faithfully. Different strategies may be employed. At times, a pastor may need to do basic grammatical instruction: "You are not using the language of sin properly. Here is what Christians mean by sin; this is what we do with that language." At other times, a pastor may work indirectly, helping others to correct their own language by asking questions or by restating something with better (theological) "grammar." In all of these approaches, the purpose of the pastor is to enable others to learn the language of the faith.

Perhaps the most difficult setting in which to teach the language of the faith is "business" meetings. The very language, of course, betrays us. Is not worship the real "business" of the church? Does not the word *business* throw us into the language of the market, strategic planning, and the like?[7] Here I confess that much work is still to be done. Perhaps we could begin by considering how the language of spiritual gifts might enter into our conduct of church meetings and correct our language and our grammar.[8]

Up to this point I have been writing as if the only thing that we did with language was speak it. However, Lindbeck's and Holmer's accounts remind us that language and practices are inextricably tied together. For example, Christian language about sin should guide us into confession, repentance, and forgiveness. That is, describing an act as sin tells us what to do with it as followers of Jesus Christ.

So we must add to our account of the pastor as language teacher: pastors must not only speak the language of faith, they must also practice it. While knowledge of the original languages, history, and culture of the Bible are important, "one suspects that it is far more important than most historical material to learn to hunger and thirst for righteousness, to learn to love a neighbor, and to achieve a high

7. See the wonderful essay by Philip D. Kenneson, "Selling [Out] the Church in the Marketplace of Desire," *Modern Theology* 9 (October 1993): 319–48.

8. One place to begin thinking about this is John Howard Yoder, "The Hermeneutics of Peoplehood," in *The Priestly Kingdom* (Notre Dame, IN: University of Notre Dame Press, 1984), 15–45.

degree of self-concern, in order to understand the religious themes of the New Testament."[9] So the character of a pastor and his or her spiritual life are crucial to rightly knowing and teaching the language of the faith. One may speak *about* forgiveness without knowing forgiveness, but one may only speak *of* forgiveness (in Holmer's terms) if one has also experienced it. Perhaps our theology, and even pastoral ministry, comes into question because we speak so often in the "about" mood.

Now this is, to be sure, a complex claim. Certainly some, perhaps many, have come to faith through the preaching of those whose character is less than admirable. Moreover, unfaithfulness does not destroy the truth of the gospel. But Paul's admonitions to Timothy and his description of his own practices make it clear that character is crucial to faithful pastoral work. And as Holmer argues, we need faithful lives to vivify, to embody, the language of the faith.[10]

We may bring together the question of character and the pastor as grammarian and language teacher by reflecting on ministry in times of grief. When a pastor sits with parents who are grieving the loss of a child, he or she may hear many "ungrammatical" statements. The pastor needs compassion and practical wisdom to respond appropriately. This is not the time for a grammar lesson; it is not the time to say, "Let me tell you how to talk properly about this event and your feelings." But it may be the time for a pastor to gently speak the language of faith and in doing so teach the grief stricken how to refer their grief to God. In this situation, correct theology and technique are not enough; the character of a pastor is also crucial.

So Lindbeck and Holmer teach us to think about the Christian community as a place where we are taught the practices and the language that witness to the gospel and enable us to live ever more faithful to the gospel. In this community, the pastor is one who teaches and guards the grammar and language of the faith. In order to do this, pastors must practice that language faithfully in their own lives.

9. Holmer, *Grammar of Faith*, 9.

10. In the next section of this chapter I will further develop this assertion by arguing that we need more than faithful pastors in order to learn the language of the faith.

Examples

In order to get clearer about this notion of the pastor as language teacher, I want to explore three examples from Roy Bell's ministry. Roy Bell is an Irishman educated in England who spent most of his adult life in ministry in Canada. After a relatively brief pastorate in New Brunswick, Roy pastored several churches in Alberta and British Columbia; he also served the Baptist Union of Western Canada and the Baptist World Alliance in several significant ways. He has been a mentor to my wife and me. Perhaps his most significant pastorate was First Baptist Church, Vancouver, from which I take most of my examples. Although Roy is aware of his own failures and shortcomings and may be somewhat embarrassed by my account, I can think of no better way to honor his ministry and develop my suggestion than by showing how Roy taught the language of the gospel in his own ministry. By so doing, I also want to emphasize the point that I am not trying to add something to pastoral ministry. I am simply trying to make more explicit and intentional something that many already do.

One of the most powerful expressions of the pastor as language teacher in Roy's ministry was his preaching. I used to complain occasionally (to Roy) that there was not enough "theology" or exegesis in his sermons. At the same time, I was puzzled by the power of his sermons. I now think that when I complained, I was complaining that in his sermons he did not directly and explicitly teach the grammar of theology. Rather, he simply put the language of the gospel to work in ways that made sense of our lives according to the gospel. Instead of telling us "what the Bible said," he taught us how to think with the Bible. He taught us how to use the language of sin and redemption in relation to our lives. He did not just tell us that the Bible calls us to be reconciled; he taught us how to practice reconciliation in our relationships with God and others. In Lindbeck's terms, he took our world and absorbed it into the biblical world.[11]

11. Lindbeck, *Nature of Doctrine*, 118: "Typology does not make scriptural contents into metaphors for extrascriptural realities, but the other way around. It does not suggest, as is often said in our day, that believers find their stories in the Bible, but rather that they make the story of the Bible their story. The cross is not to be viewed as a figurative representation for suffering nor the messianic kingdom as a symbol for hope in the future; rather, suffering

One example of this is Roy's sermon series "True and False Guilt." In this series, Roy took the language of guilt and taught us how to use it properly. Just as in cooking we must not confuse baking soda and arsenic, so in Christianity we must learn not to confuse true and false guilt. In his sermons, Roy helped us discern the ways in which we wrongly use the language of guilt to refer to actions and feelings. He taught us that we often misuse the language of guilt to describe actions and circumstances over which we have no control, in which we are the victims of sin rather than the perpetrators. As victims, we wrongly apply guilt to ourselves. Such wrong usage condemns us to frustration, despair, and even abandonment of the faith.

Then he taught us how rightly to use the language of guilt, so that we might know forgiveness and freedom. In this instance, we must learn to acknowledge that we are not only victims of sin but also its perpetrators. This is true guilt and can be properly dealt only by confession, repentance, and forgiveness on the way to reconciliation. Only by learning how to properly use the language of guilt can we know what to do about it—what practice to engage.[12]

Another aspect of Roy's preaching exemplifies what I am arguing: his use of biography. Roy uses biography not to illustrate a point but to show how lives embody languages and practices. This is a subtle but important distinction. To use a life to illustrate a point is to assume that the point is most important and life is incidental to ideas or principles or sermon points. Consciously or not, Roy uses biography in a way that simply shows us how a life embodies the language and practice of the faith. A way of life faithful to the gospel is the point. This is why Roy's sermons seldom had "points." In fact, one could despair of trying to nail down the point or points of his sermons. Rather, the whole language of a sermon and the life it inscribed was "the point."

Apart from his sermons, Roy was also an effective language teacher in personal encounters. The most direct and formative experience I

---

should be cruciform, and hopes for the future messianic. . . . It is the text, so to speak, which absorbs the world, rather than the world the text." See also Bruce D. Marshall, "Absorbing the World," in *Theology and Dialogue: Essays in Conversation with George Lindbeck*, ed. Bruce D. Marshall (Notre Dame, IN: University of Notre Dame Press, 1990), 69–102.

12. See my exploration of the distinction between victim and perpetrator of sin in Jonathan R. Wilson, *God So Loved the World: A Christology for Disciples* (Grand Rapids: Baker, 2001), 91–97 and 109–115.

had of this aspect of Roy's ministry was my learning how to use the language of the faith to think about and practice power. My own Christian tradition had left me ill equipped for speaking faithfully about power. The exercise of power, I had been told, was sinful in itself. As a consequence, in my early experience of the church, the unavoidable exercise of power was governed by vicious, worldly practices, since that was the only language we had for talking about power. Roy, in many conversations about church meetings, denominational politics, and the like, forced me to begin to develop faithful language and practices for the exercise of power. Of course, we remain sinners and all fall short, but I believe that Roy's own ministry represents a commitment to seek to bring even the exercise of power under the rule of Jesus Christ, not under the rule of my ambitions and schemes, nor anyone else's.

Roy occasionally lamented his tendency toward ruthlessness, but in doing so he drew on the language of faith to help keep his exercise of power in check. It is the pastor or other leader who has no language of faith to apply to power who is most in danger of using it abusively. Roy recognized the necessity of power to bring change to a congregation, to accomplish the ministry and mission of the church, and to transform lives. But at his best, he aligned his exercise of power with the *telos* of ministry so that he sought not an external good but greater participation in the church's *telos*. (We will return to the "practice" of power in chapter 10.)

Implications

Up to this point I have developed my account of the pastor as language teacher by looking at a variety of sources and practices that may illuminate pastoral ministry among the people of God. This way of thinking has innumerable implications for the life and witness of the people of God. I will draw out three.

First, thinking of the pastor as language teacher helps us see why we need pastors. We need pastors because we need people with the intellectual and spiritual capacity to teach and guard the grammar and language of the faith. Pastors are those whom the church has identified as having those capacities. Further, pastors are those for whom the church has set aside time so that they may attend carefully to the grammar of the faith and to our language. As the people of God carry out their myriad responsibilities, pastors help us learn the language and sustain the practices that enable us to live as faithful servants of God and witnesses to God's work in Jesus Christ.

This approach helps us understand, in part, the substance and purpose of theological education. When we study the Bible, Hebrew and Greek, ancient history and culture, our interests are not antiquarian. Rather, we are apprenticing ourselves to the biblical world so that we may speak the language of the gospel more faithfully today. So to know "what the scholars say" is not an end in itself; it is worthwhile only to the extent that it enables faithful speech and practice. Let me go one step further, for it seems to me that much biblical scholarship seems to be caught up in the language of academia and has very little to do with faithfulness to the cultural-linguistic world of the gospel.[13]

As with biblical studies, when we study theology—the early christological controversies, John Calvin's *Institutes*, John Wesley's *Sermons*, Karl Barth's *Dogmatics*, Donald Bloesch's *Foundations*—we are not just learning what they taught. Rather, we are again apprenticing ourselves, learning with them the grammatical and linguistic errors that have been made, and learning how the language of the faith has been spoken faithfully by others. We may also rediscover vocabulary that we have neglected and need to recover today.

Admittedly, we do not often think of theological education in this way. Nor do we have many theologians who represent this approach to theology. Indeed, one may discern an underlying but growing tension among evangelical theologians over Lindbeck's proposal and its impact on evangelical theology. Nevertheless, I think that there is much promise in this account for the future faithfulness of the church to the gospel of Jesus Christ.

Finally, in theological education we may begin to understand what we should be doing in other courses, such as counseling, evangelism, and interdisciplinary studies. Here too we may think of ourselves as teaching the language and practices of the gospel in these areas of life.

13. See my further argument along this line in Jonathan R. Wilson, "Theology and the Old Testament," in *Interpreting the Old Testament: A Guide to Exegesis*, ed. Craig C. Broyles (Grand Rapids: Baker, 2001), 245–64.

In fact, further thought here might enable us to give a more coherent account of theological education than we currently have.

So we need pastors as language teachers. But a second implication of thinking of pastors as language teachers is that pastors are not all that we need in order to learn the language of the faith. Think again of how we learn a natural language. Most who have French as their first language learned it by growing up within a community that spoke French. At some point more formal education in French took place through schooling in the history and grammar of the language. And supporting all of this are the great works of French literature, such as Blaise Pascal's *Provincial Letters* and the novels of Gustave Flaubert and Victor Hugo. In other words, teachers of grammar and language are not always themselves the best speakers and the greatest artists of the language. Eventually, we learn a language by attending to acknowledged masters of the language.

In the same way, pastors and theologians may not be the best speakers of the language. They will often be dependent on the work—and lives—of others. As I noted above, this is one of the reasons we study the work of past masters. But we also need to extend this into the present. In every congregation I have known, there have been people of God who have quietly and profoundly spoken the language of the gospel in their lives—at work, at home, and at church. These are the saints of the church from whom a pastor can learn much. They are current and local "masters" of the language of the gospel who will never write a book but whose lives are masterpieces.

In my own pastorate, I learned much about the proper Christian language of grief from a young couple whose son died shortly after birth. I learned much about faithfulness in "ordinary" jobs from two men who shared their lives with me. And I have learned much about faithful language in the home from both my wife and my daughter. It is not always appropriate to name examples, but sermons may often be covert meditations on the faithful life of one of these saints. Likewise, in counseling I have often drawn not on what I know but on what others have modeled for me as they have used the language of the gospel to interpret their experiences of abuse, of moral failure, of emotional turmoil.

The third implication of this account of the pastor as language teacher may be brought into view by reflecting on the way that our use of "natural" languages deteriorates. For example, my use of English in everyday conversation is often ungrammatical. As hard as I try, I say "different than" instead of "different from," and catchphrases such as "like," "I mean," and "you know" creep into my vocabulary. The specialized uses that we have learned for natural languages also deteriorate. For example, several years ago I was an engineer on an oil-fired steam locomotive. My everyday language involved atomizers, injectors, the water glass, and the fuel handle. But now, several years later, my ability to use that language properly has faded. I had to think long and hard to recall that the "thing" (language deteriorates!) that creates the draft up a smokestack is called the blower.

In the same way, our ability to use the language of faith deteriorates. Under the pressure of our everyday lives, we cease to use the language of gratitude, we no longer use *sin* to describe our disobedience to God, and we do not bless those who persecute us. In place of this language, we use the language of politics (we have rights), of psychotherapy (we have complexes), of economics (we are owed).

Worship as Practice

The place where we gather to relearn and correct our language is worship. Among many other things, worship is a concentrated lesson in the language of faith. Here, for example, we relearn the language of sin. As C. S. Lewis says somewhere in his writings, sometimes we say the confession because we truly are aware of our sin; other times we say the confession in order to learn that we are "miserable sinners." Of course, the Christian language of sin goes further: what we do with sin is confess it and then receive forgiveness from a merciful and loving God. So the language of sin teaches us how to think of ourselves and of God: we are sinners who have been forgiven by God's mercy in Jesus Christ.

In worship we also learn the language of thankfulness. All that we have and are comes as gifts from God. So as we gather up our praise we are taught not to think of these things as "ours," to do with as we please, but as God's, to do with as God pleases. We can no longer hold onto our success, our prosperity, our status, as our right or as what we deserve. Rather, we learn to describe them as gifts to be passed on to others.

As we gather up our confession and our thanksgiving in worship, we may also bring our misery and our need. Often in everyday life we are very disciplined at keeping our needs to ourselves. A confession of weakness or uncertainty in our job can lead to all sorts of unpleasant consequences. We very easily and often carry this discipline over into our relationship with God. But as the congregation is led in worship to share our needs with one another and with God, we are once again learning the proper language and practice for referring our needs to the gospel.

Finally, in worship all of our language and practices together teach us what the world really looks like and is according to the gospel. In worship, our language and our practices train us for living more faithfully in a world full of rebellion, full of other languages and practices. Those who lead in worship must give concentrated attention to the use of language and practices that correct our errors and enable us to participate in the real world of the gospel.

Although this account runs the danger of making it seem that worship is a practice session for real life, at its best it can help us see how to heal the breach between "worship" and the rest of life. In this account, all of life is to be lived in service and praise to God. What we call "worship," that gathered time of the community, is the time we set aside for single-minded concentration on and training in how we should always be living. What we say and do in worship is what we should say and do in all of our lives.

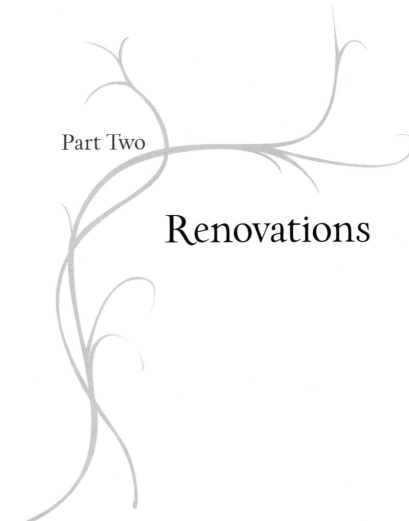

Part Two

Renovations

6

Witness as Kingdom Words and Deeds

or many years I taught the life and mission of the church by using the image of "journey inward, journey outward."[1] This image helps us see that the life of the church follows a double rhythm or movement. I found this "doubling" especially helpful when I developed the image as a heartbeat: the heart beats once to draw the blood in for oxygenation and then out to circulate blood through the body, delivering oxygen and other life essentials. Though I still use the image and find it helpful, recently I have also recognized its limitations, because the church's life is energized in the midst of "circulating" in the world as well as in gathering together. Likewise, the mission of the church is fulfilled when it gathers for worship and instruction as well as when it goes into the world to serve.

My recent recognition of the limitations of "journey inward, journey outward" is especially important as this chapter brings into focus the practice of witness. Having centered our attention on God in the practices of the church (chaps. 2–4) and then considered the role of the pastor in the practicing church, it is now time to bring the community and its witness into focus. The community, of course, has never been absent from my account, and I have already noted some of the issues that we will consider in this chapter. Moreover,

---

1. I am uncertain now, but I may have learned this image from Elizabeth O'Connor, *Journey Inward, Journey Outward* (New York: Harper and Row, 1968).

witness is carried on in the midst of worship as a sign to the world of God's worthiness of praise as we declare God's character and work and live it out in our practices of worship. But now the purpose of this chapter is to bring the practice of witness out of the background and onto center stage.

To do this, I will first argue for the importance of the *community* called to witness. Too often we have treated witness as a solo act rather than a communal act. In the New Testament, witness is centered in the life of the community. Then I will develop the claim that the *telos* of witness is the kingdom of God. This claim illuminates the practice of witness and leads to the consideration of one perennial controversy in the church's witness: the relative importance of "evangelism" and "social action" in the church's witness. I will argue that the *telos* of the kingdom dissolves this tension and removes the bewitchment that this debate often casts over the church. Having removed that obstacle, I will turn finally to a brief and suggestive account of how the various practices of the church bear witness to the kingdom of God. I will devote an entire later chapter to one other aspect of the church's witness: the power that the church received when the Holy Spirit came and the power that continues to come by the Spirit.

Community

I begin with the importance of community not because it is the first or most important part of the commission that Jesus gave, though both may be argued. Rather, I begin with community because this aspect is the most neglected and least recognized. When Jesus commissions his disciples, he commissions them as a whole, not as individuals. Certainly we see Peter, Paul, and other individuals preaching, but even that act of witness is an act of the whole church through their common life.

This plurality of commissioning and indeed of the New Testament is obscured for us today by the limitations of contemporary English. In the English that we use today, we have no clear second person plural. *You* refers both to a singular "you" and a plural "you." Now, having grown up in the southern United States, I am quite familiar with the possibilities of "y'all." And I've also heard "youse" and "youse guys." But none of those colloquialisms will ever be sufficiently recognized to help us recover the you-plural. Moreover, these terms are often used casually for the singular as well as the plural.

This limitation is extremely unfortunate, because most of the New Testament passages that are addressed to "you" are plural in the original Greek. Previous users of English had an alternative. The English that is used for the King James (or Authorized) Version of the Bible reflects the plural you with the word *ye* when it is in the subject position in a sentence. (*Ye* changes to *you* when it is in an object of a verb or preposition.) Consider the following verses:

> But seek ye first the kingdom of God, and his righteousness; and all these things shall be added unto you. (Matt. 6:33)

> Go ye therefore, and teach all nations, baptizing them in the name of the Father, and of the Son, and of the Holy Ghost. (Matt. 28:19)

> And ye are witnesses of these things. (Luke 24:48)

> But ye shall receive power, after that the Holy Ghost is come upon you: and ye shall be witnesses unto me both in Jerusalem, and in all Judaea, and in Samaria, and unto the uttermost part of the earth. (Acts 1:8)

These promises and commands of Jesus are given to "you plural"—the community that is the people of God. This focus on community is essential to the argument of this book, because the life of a community is essential to learning a language and engaging in practices. The elements of a language may be memorized in solitude, but speaking a language requires others with whom the language forms a common life and enables the structures and activities of life to take place. Indeed, language skills and community participation and formation go together.

We may understand this better by returning to the example of basketball. A "community" is formed by a basketball team as players learn a language for defensive schemes (man-to-man, match-up zone, box-and-one, triangle-and-two), offensive schemes (pick-and-roll, post-up, high post, low post, motion, backdoor cut), and individual moves (skip pass, bounce pass, jump hook, screen, double-screen, alley-oop). A basketball team is a community for which this language refers to something and enables actions to be described and events to take place.

Similarly, the very nature of the gospel requires community for witness by living out the practices and language of the gospel. Reconciliation, forgiveness, restoration, praise, thanksgiving, and so much more have their beginning in God's gracious act in Jesus Christ. But as human beings are called into Christ, none of these actions can be contained in a relationship merely between God and the individual. In every part of the Old Testament and New Testament, the call of any individual is to and for the community.

We see this clearly in the call of Abraham, whom God blesses by making his descendants a nation and through them blessing all the people of the earth. We see this in the disciples, who are called by Christ to be his witnesses and teachers as the Holy Spirit brings into existence the church. We see this in Paul, who is called by God to be a servant of the gospel to the saints in many places.[2]

This community, the people of God now called church, is one of the focal points of the New Testament. The Gospels give an account of the training of the first disciples in the practice of community formation. The Sermon on the Mount is a well-known and clear example of this community formation. Its address is not to individuals who heroically follow the way of Christ in solitude. Nor is the intention of the Sermon to demonstrate how each of us fails to measure up and thus needs God's forgiveness. Rather, the Sermon is a description of and call to the communal life made possible by God's grace made known in Jesus Christ by the Holy Spirit. In John's Gospel, we read of the climax of this training in community formation when Jesus tells the first disciples, "By this everyone will know that you are my disciples, if you have love for one another" (John 13:35). For Paul, the *telos* of God's work, God's ultimate

2. This is made clear in the way that Lesslie Newbigin develops one meaning of the biblical notion of election. See Lesslie Newbigin, *The Open Secret: Sketches for a Missionary Theology*, rev. ed. (Grand Rapids: Eerdmans, 1995). George R. Hunsberger describes the significance of election for Newbigin in *Bearing the Witness of the Spirit: Lesslie Newbigin's Theology of Cultural Plurality* (Grand Rapids: Eerdmans, 1998), chap. 2.

purpose through the work of Christ, is the new creation for which God is forming a new community that is reconciled to God and to one another (Ephesians).[3]

Kingdom

The church is not incidental to the salvation of individuals, nor is it merely the instrument of salvation for individuals. Rather, the church is integral to the ultimate intention of God to redeem creation. That ultimate intention (*telos*) is so rich in significance that it cannot be captured by one term. Given that warning, however, we may represent that richness in different contexts with a term or image appropriate to each particular context. In this context, the *telos* of the gospel is well represented by the image of the kingdom of God. This image fits well because we are working in the context of the new community in the new creation. These two aspects can be brought together by the image of the kingdom, when the kingdom is understood as something more than the human community. The kingdom is the human community alive forever in the context of a new creation redeemed by the work of Christ.

The church has often used other terms and images to identify its witness. We may speak of "witnessing to Christ" or "bearing witness to the gospel." But *kingdom of God* is a phrase deeply rooted in Jesus's own witness and in the life of the early church after Christ's death and resurrection. In Luke's account of the resurrected Christ, he tells us that "after [Christ's] suffering he presented himself alive to [the disciples] by many convincing proofs, appearing to them during forty days and speaking about the kingdom of God" (Acts 1:3). And although we do not read a lot about the kingdom of God in Paul's letters, Luke makes it clear that the kingdom of God was central to Paul's witness. When Luke summarizes the work of Paul in Ephesus, he describes Paul "arguing persuasively about the kingdom of God" (Acts 19:8 TNIV). As the book of Acts closes with Paul in Rome, Luke announces that "for two whole years Paul

---

3. "Cross, Community, New Creation" is a summary of themes found in Richard Hays, *The Moral Vision of the New Testament* (San Francisco: HarperSanFrancisco, 1999).

stayed there in his own rented house and welcomed all who came to see him. He proclaimed the kingdom of God and taught about the Lord Jesus Christ—with all boldness and without hindrance!" (Acts 28:30–31 TNIV).

The church is the witness to and servant of that kingdom. Before we consider how the practices of the people of God proclaim the kingdom, we must first be clear about the relationship between the church and the kingdom. The church participates in the kingdom and anticipates the kingdom, but the kingdom is larger than the church and is not yet fully present in the church or the world. The kingdom is larger than the church because the kingdom is the redemption of all creation. God's work in Christ is not merely for the redemption of human beings; it is for the redemption of all creation. The kingdom is also larger than the church because the kingdom is already present but not yet fully present.[4] Thus, even as the church bears witness to the kingdom, it falls short of the fullness of the kingdom.

When the church loses sight of its distance from the kingdom, bad things happen. Sometimes the church loses sight simply by neglect, sometimes by more actively denying its distance from the kingdom. When the church loses this distinction, one of its tendencies is to deny its own failures, its own sin. This happens when the church thinks that it has to *be* the kingdom rather than bear witness to the kingdom. At this point, the church begins to justify itself and deny its wrongdoing.

Another tendency of the church is to claim that the true church is invisible rather than visible. That is, when the visible church clearly falls short of the kingdom, we fall back on the claim that the "true church" is invisible. If we could only see this church, then we would see a church that is faultless.

But both of these tendencies eventually lead the church into a situation where its own life no longer witnesses to the kingdom of God. The choice is not between a visible church that claims to be the kingdom by denying its own sin and an invisible church that is faithful to the kingdom but cannot be seen and thus cannot wit-

4. See my development of this theme in Jonathan R. Wilson, *God So Loved the World: A Christology for Disciples* (Grand Rapids: Baker, 2001), chap. 7.

ness to the kingdom. There is another choice, one that is biblically faithful: a visible church that witnesses to the kingdom by aligning its practices with the kingdom. These practices include faithfulness that reflects the righteousness of the kingdom, but they also include confession that reflects the grace of the kingdom and the distance of the church from the coming fullness of the kingdom.

So as we further explore the practices of the church as witness to the kingdom, we must maintain three subtle and crucial convictions: (1) the church proclaims the kingdom in the practices that form the life of the church, (2) the church participates in the (incomplete) presence of the kingdom, and (3) the church is not the fullness of the kingdom.

The Practice of Witness

One perennial controversy in the recent history of the church is the relative energy directed toward two aspects of the church's witness: evangelism and social action. In this debate, evangelism has been understood as a "spiritual" activity—the work of presenting the gospel so that people are persuaded to put their faith in Jesus Christ. Social action has been understood as the "material" work of making a better society that brings about human flourishing through such work as feeding the hungry, liberating the oppressed, and educating the ignorant.

This debate has been worked over many times—to the point of becoming predictable and tiresome in many cases. My intention here is not to work through it once again but to bring the notion of practice to bear on the issues that are raised in the debate. By doing so, I hope to illuminate why the debate has been so intractable and to set out a way of thinking about these issues that opens up more understanding of how the church needs to carry out its commission.

To accomplish that goal, I must review briefly the way the debate has unfolded. One of the reasons the debate has been so difficult is that both positions can claim biblical support for their argument. In the best of times, the advocates on all sides have recognized this biblical basis, and the argument has been about the relative importance to place on activities within a particular social setting. For example, in a society where the church is well established and has a long history, the cause of Christ may (some would argue) be better served by social action than by evangelism. In this case the argument centers on strategy and context. At other times, the arguments have become arguments about the very nature of Christian faith and the mission of the church.

In all these various circumstances, some basic positions may be staked out.

Evangelism only. Advocates of this position may not deny the importance of alleviating people's misery and improving their physical circumstances, but they argue that those tasks may be accomplished by many different groups. Only the church has the message of eternal salvation through faith in Jesus Christ. So when the church directs any of its talent and energy toward something other than delivering that message, it is being diverted from the one thing that only the church can do.

Social action only. Advocates of this position typically argue that we should leave the destiny of others in God's hands. This is often connected to an implicit or explicit conviction that through God's sovereignty and mercy everyone will be saved. So the task of the church is to alleviate suffering and work for justice today. In that way we bear witness to the perfect kingdom in which we will all live one day.

Evangelism leads to social action. Advocates of this position argue that the first step toward alleviating suffering and working for justice is to change people's hearts. When people's hearts are changed, they will be more compassionate and caring and, therefore, engage in social action.

Social action leads to evangelism. Advocates of this approach may be represented by the familiar claim that "no one can hear the gospel on an empty stomach." The empty stomach could be replaced with almost any oppressive or unjust social circumstance. The key here is that one's basic needs must be met before one can think about other needs—such as eternal life. Or the argument may be that social action wins the church the right to be heard.

Evangelism and social action in partnership. Advocates of this position strive to maintain an overall balance between these two activities. Any "social action" must have an "evangelism" component and vice versa. Such balance may be achieved over time rather than in any one activity. Practitioners of this approach do not slavishly follow some formula, but they do seek to be wise in achieving these two goals.

These five approaches roughly represent the various voices that have been heard in this debate through recent years. They help us see the challenges in being faithful to the gospel in varying circumstances as we interpret those circumstances. But in the end, they all misconstrue the church's commission to witness to the kingdom of God, because they lead us into an argument over "getting people saved" versus "making people's lives better." Even if we are clever enough to answer that both are part of the church's mission, we have made a mistake because we have accepted a faulty premise.

To correct this error, we must think of the church's mission modeled in Jesus's own ministry. He has simply commissioned us to continue the work that he initiated. Certainly there is an unbridgeable gap between his life, death, and resurrection and our witness to it, but we are to continue Jesus's work by the power of the Holy Spirit. The work that Jesus calls us to is to bear witness to the kingdom of God and call people to life in that kingdom (life in Christ) by our words and our deeds.

This insight—words and deeds as witness to the kingdom—makes it possible to correct the mistakes in the debate over evangelism and social action. We tend to think of evangelism as speech and social action as deeds. But what we need to do is recognize that both our words and our deeds call people to life in the kingdom through faith in Jesus Christ. Our actions as much as our words bear witness to the kingdom. Jesus's words and his deeds proclaim the kingdom of God; so should ours.

We tend also to think of evangelism as pertaining to "spiritual life" and social action as pertaining to "material (or physical) life." This distinction, if accepted as the terms for debate, misconstrues the nature of the kingdom and of faith in Christ. The kingdom of God does not admit any division of the spiritual from the physical. We may distinguish these, but we cannot separate them. And in practice of witness, the church must embrace the fullness of the kingdom. We are witnessing to the kingdom when we care for someone's bodily needs just as fully as when we talk to them about a "change of heart." In Jesus's own ministry the interconnection between healing one's body and forgiving sins reveals this powerfully.

Finally, and most important, to construe the debate in terms of "evangelism versus social action" turns our vision from the proper *telos* of the church's mission. We must keep our eyes fixed on the work of Christ in our world—the kingdom that has arrived but is not yet fully present in this age. No matter how we work out the balance between evangelism and social action, these two direct our attention in the wrong directions. If we focus on evangelism, then we tend to look for the growth of the church as the sign of faithfulness. If we focus on social action, then we tend to look for political change as the sign of our faithfulness. To be sure, the growth of the church and political change may be good things. But they are not indubitable signs of our faithfulness and of the presence of the kingdom. In the same way that prosperity may or may not be a sign of one's righteousness, so too growth and change may or may not be signs of the kingdom. We must not mistake the possible sign for the real presence of the kingdom. And the debate over evangelism and social action tends to do just that—bewitch us with the penultimate rather than the ultimate.

Witness in Word and Deed

The recognition that the mission of the church is witness to the kingdom in word and deed corrects the misconstrued debate over evangelism and social action. The energy and commitment that are often dissipated by the tug of war between these two are properly directed and liberated by the *telos* of witness to the kingdom.

At the same time, "witness to the kingdom in word and deed" directs us to the necessity of community for this practice. To say that the community is necessary to the practice of witness is not a trite claim that when a follower of Jesus visits someone in prison he must do so in a group. Nor is it the claim that when someone presents the call to faith in Christ and life in the kingdom she must always do so in company with other believers. Rather, the assertion of the necessity of community for the practice of kingdom witness is the call to recognize that the practice of the kingdom is so radically at odds with the life of this age and the kingdom of death that only a community can sustain faithful witness. The life to which Jesus calls us in the Sermon on the Mount is not the life of a solitary hero of the spiritual life; the life to which Jesus calls us is the life of a community: "Seek *ye* first the kingdom of God . . . *Ye* are witnesses of these things . . . Go *ye* . . ."

So when one person from the disciple community visits someone in prison, she does so with the prayer support of the community. And that same community participates with her in processing the questions of justice, forgiveness, and reconciliation that arise from such ministry in the context of the kingdom of God, which teaches us to hunger and thirst for righteousness. Likewise, when one person calls another to faith in Christ, he does so knowing that there is an entire community of disciples in which new life will be nourished and guided. When we understand well the practice of witness to the kingdom, even isolation and separation cannot break the communal practice of such witness. If a follower of Jesus Christ is jailed for his faith and another is hospitalized for illness, they are not removed from the community. Rather, when the community remembers them in prayer, those supposedly isolated and separated individuals are re-membered by the community through the practice of prayer, which is one of the signs that the kingdom is not limited by space and time.

We often stumble over this truth of the kingdom in our overly individualistic and materialistic culture. We think of ministry in terms of individuals, and we think of presence in strictly physical terms. But if we submit ourselves to the world of the Bible, then we must begin to recognize that space and time do not break apart the Christian community. Rather, Christian community is broken by sinful alienation and forgetfulness. This brokenness can be healed by the reconciling work of the Spirit. And across space and time we can be present with one another by prayer and burden bearing through the power of the Holy Spirit. Our daily and weekly prayers for those who are ill and "shut-in" should be more explicitly tied to the practice of re-membering through brief prefatory comments. Taking the Eucharist to the sick, as many churches do, is an opportunity for correcting our individualism and recovering the corporate character of witness. The recently renewed attention to the "persecuted church" crosses space and time as we seek to bear others' burdens with them.

We need to give greater attention to this in other practices of witness beyond the Christian community. When we send people out into the community as volunteers at a soup kitchen, as advocates for the homeless, as servants of those in need, as people declaring the good news of Jesus Christ and inviting others to believe, do we view these activities as practices of the community that require teams or bands of disciples? Or do we simply announce certain needs and opportunities for ministry and leave individuals to find their own way into them? Do we see that witness to the kingdom, in whatever expression, is a practice of the kingdom that requires a community?

This call to witness to the kingdom in word and deed may not add new practices to the mission of the church. Instead, it gives direction and meaning to all the practices of the church. That direction and meaning should not always be explicit and intentional, but at some level the disciple community should have those who are being reflective about how the various practices of the church witness to the kingdom.[5]

The call to "word and deed" reminds us that the kingdom to which we witness is not merely a set of ideas or list of propositions; the kingdom is creation redeemed. It is to this reality, established by the Son and empowered by the Spirit, that we are called and commissioned. Words that witness to the kingdom are themselves acts that direct our vision toward the presence of the kingdom. Deeds are visible words that participate in the reality of the kingdom that is present for the redemption of the world.

---

5. One of the best examples of this sort of reflection is James Wm. McLendon Jr., with Nancey Murphy, *Witness*, vol. 3 of *Systematic Theology* (Nashville: Abingdon, 2000).

7

Discipleship as Human Flourishing

*J*esus commissions the church to go and make disciples. Discipleship is typically one of the activities to which the church commits itself. But at times the church has tended to disconnect the work of disciplemaking from the activities of evangelism and conversion. At these times, the church behaves as if the real mission of the church is to get people to a onetime event that "converts" them to faith, erases their guilt, and guarantees their salvation for eternity. None of the language that I used in the previous sentence is necessarily wrong. It is all language that communicates something true about the good news of Jesus Christ. But everything in that sentence—converting to Christ, erasing guilt, and eternal salvation—is wrong, devastatingly wrong, when it is disconnected from the *telos* that gives it proper meaning and direction.

The *telos* that gives meaning and direction to the language of conversion, faith, eternal life, being born again, and other language familiar to Christians is the kingdom of God proclaimed, enacted, and embodied by Jesus Christ. When we lose sight of the proper *telos* for conversion, faith, forgiveness, eternal life, and other claims for the gospel, that very biblical language miscommunicates the call to the kingdom of God and faith in Christ. That miscommunication happens both within the life of the church and in the church's witness to the world. Our impulse is to abandon the language of conversion, faith, and so on when we recognize the miscommunication that is taking place. But following that impulse is a mistake, because in erasing that vocabulary we lose the truth to which it points. Instead of erasing the language, we need to correct it by redirecting it toward the kingdom of God.

In this chapter, I will explore how miscommunication takes shape and how we can correct it by rediscovering the language and practice of discipleship. We will begin with an account of our present cultural context that identifies some of the obstacles in the way of recovering the *telos* of the kingdom and the practice of discipleship. These obstacles subtly distort both the internal life of the church and the church's witness. Thus, we must understand them in order to recover the proper language and the practice of discipleship that corrects our misunderstanding and miscommunication of the gospel.

Cultural Context

Our present cultural context is marked by an absence and active denial of any *telos* for human life. The denial of a *telos* takes on subtle characteristics in our culture. This denial is not identical to the denial of purpose or meaning. In our culture, we may assert that we can find purpose and meaning, but we think that such purpose and meaning are found by human effort. Or more often, that purpose and meaning are created by human beings. Or finally, that purpose and meaning are chosen by individuals who are free to choose from a range of possibilities. None of these is what I mean by *telos*. Rather, *telos* means that purpose and meaning are *given* in the very nature of who we are as human beings. But the gospel goes beyond that, to declare that we can know our *telos* only by the gift of knowledge that comes to us through Jesus Christ. That is why it is gospel: good news. It is news because it tells us something that we otherwise do not know; it is good because it tells us who we are made to be and how to be that which we are made to be. So for the church *telos* is not something we find but something we receive; not something we create but something for which we are created; not something we choose from a range of possibilities but the one possibility that we are free to choose only as God enables us.

Again, such an understanding of *telos* runs contrary to our present context, which understands human freedom in terms of an absolute freedom to decide one's own end and which further interprets any claim that our *telos* is given and revealed as an imposition of dominance and veiled exercise of power over others. That understanding persists in both the cultural context called modernity and the one called postmodernity.

In modernity, the teleology of the gospel appears to be a denial of human freedom from rule by another, the displacement of autonomy (self-rule) by heteronomy (other-rule). One characteristic of modernity is its enshrining autonomy as essential to our cultural identity. Autonomy means that humans are free to choose their own ends. Thus, much of modernity may be understood as the human effort to harness the natural world through human abilities so that we control our own destinies.

The way we use science and develop technology reflects this quest. Humankind has always had sciences and technologies, but in modernity those sciences and technologies have been refined and tied to an ateleological approach to life that reflects the conviction that we are in control. In modernity, we maximize our control in order to maximize our freedom to determine our own destinies.

As we will see in more detail below, this construal of freedom in modernity places value on consumer choice, increasing one's options, and maintaining control of one's own life. The call to become disciples of Jesus Christ and live in light of the kingdom of God does not sound much like news, nor does it sound good, to modern ears. As a consequence, we often modify the gospel and suppress or discard the call to discipleship in order to make faith in Christ attractive to those whose sensibilities are shaped by modernity.

At the same time that modernity shapes much of contemporary life, its failings and illusions are being exposed. One way to describe the recognition that the influence of modernity is beginning to wane is to talk about the shift to postmodernity. There are many debated meanings for *postmodernity*; here I use the word simply to refer to the cultural shift marked by the breakdown of modernity. That makes postmodernity largely negative at this point: "not modernity" or "after modernity." To give it some context, I use *postmodernity* to refer to the loss of confidence in human ability to discover or create meaning for life. Postmodernity is the reluctant recognition that human beings do not have the freedom to choose their own destinies by controlling nature through technology.

In postmodernity, human beings are left with power but not meaning. Thus, the power we humans exercise serves no great purpose. In some literature this "great purpose" is described as a metanarrative. Those shaped by modernity believe that humans are capable of constructing our own metanarrative. Those shaped by postmodernity believe that such confidence in human powers is mistaken and based on an illusion. When we strip human life of the ability to create meaning and purpose by controlling our destinies, all we are left with is the meaningless exercise of power and the purposeless quest for control. In postmodernity, then, power and control serve no purpose other than the protection of my meaningless and purposeless life, short as it may be.

In the context of postmodernity, any claim to a larger purpose is a product of self-deception or an attempt to deceive others in a quest for power, whether that claim is rooted in human accomplishment or in divine gift. If modernity is rooted in the Enlightenment as the human exodus from our self-imposed bondage, then postmodernity is our exodus from the self-deception that humans have the power and freedom to choose our destiny. We have power, but we have no destiny.

For postmodernity, then, the good news of Jesus Christ comes as a double absurdity: the gospel claims that we live in a universe that has meaning and purpose. The disciple community uses the term *creation* to bear witness to our conviction that the *telos* of the cosmos is given to it by the One who causes it to be. And the gospel of the kingdom teaches that the way to live in creation is to take all one's power and serve others in accordance with the kingdom life revealed in Jesus Christ.

Cultural Distortions

When the church neglects, fails to understand, or denies its cultural context, it runs the risk of distorting the gospel under the unrecognized influence of the culture. This challenge extends back into scripture, where we read of Jesus's own confrontations with the distortions of the religious leaders of his day and the many controversies that Paul addresses in his letters. The church knows rightly that the gospel makes sense of the cosmos and human life in the light of Jesus Christ. But this truth can be easily distorted into the practice of trimming the gospel so that it conforms to the world's sense of things.

In the context of modernity, the church has succumbed to the temptation to trim the gospel to fit human reason and autonomy. The most famous example of this is a book by Immanuel Kant, *Religion within the Bounds of Reason Alone*. In that book Kant adjusts and interprets the biblical accounts so that they fit the convictions of his day. At that point, the kingdom of God is not news, because it tells people only what they already know; nor is the kingdom good, because it adds nothing to hope for beyond human powers.

Kant's distortions are fairly obvious to us today, though many are still following that pattern of trimming the gospel of the kingdom to fit the context. More subtle are the ways that the gospel may be distorted by churches that immediately scorn Kant's approach. Even in churches that seek to conserve faithful witness to the gospel, the practice of evangelism may become distorted by the pressures of modernity.

This distortion begins in the context of modernity and its emphasis on human autonomy, freedom to choose, and breadth of choice. In response to this thirst for freedom and choice, the church appears to behave sometimes as if it is battling for "market share" in the marketplace of consumer preferences in spirituality. Christians think in terms of consumer choice about their own life in the kingdom and their knowledge of Christ. And they present the gospel of the kingdom in the same way.

As a result, evangelism looks something like shopping around for a religion the way one shops around for a car. A perfectly free human being interviews the representatives of a number of religions that he is interested in and considers all the options. He weighs the various advantages and disadvantages, the experience of other customers, satisfied and dissatisfied. (Can you imagine an Internet site with the testimonies of followers of various religions, giving one to five stars and explaining their ratings?) In the end the autonomous consumer chooses Jesus Christ. He signs a contract and, shaking Jesus's hand, says something like "Congratulations, Jesus, you have my spiritual business."

That scenario may seem bizarre, but my observation of the lives of Christians and actual presentations of the gospel confirm that something like that has become prevalent in the church. In such a practice, we suppress or even discard the biblical call to give up one's life, to submit to the rule of another, and to embrace suffering as the natural consequence of living by the kingdom in a world that is in rebellion against the kingdom. Those things can be added on later, as options. The important thing is to get the commitment.

There is a subtle distortion of an important truth in all of this. Life in the kingdom and knowledge of Jesus Christ are about one's eternal destiny. But that destiny is our *telos*, it is what we are made for, it is our purpose, our meaning, and not only ours but also the *telos* of the cosmos. So the good news of Jesus Christ is that by entry into the kingdom and knowledge of him, we begin living in that destiny now. To learn how to do that, we must become disciples.

In the context of postmodernity, the church's temptations are still developing. Not all are entirely in focus, so we must commit ourselves to vigilance. At the present time, the most obvious temptation is to present the good news merely as an invitation to join a wonderful, lively, sustaining, protective community. This temptation faces us because postmodernity turns us away from the autonomous individual and emphasizes the struggle for power among communities. Most who have postmodern sensibilities are looking for a community to join.

In this context, an invitation to join a powerful, relatively coherent community can be very appealing. The disciple community—close-knit, mutually supportive, disciplined—has obvious attractions. And the formation of a community is true to the intention of the church and the desire of many to rediscover the call to discipleship. But to present a call to community as the gospel is a betrayal of the gospel, even when it is a call to the community of disciples of Jesus Christ.

The key to the temptation is the reduction of the gospel to *nothing but* an invitation to join a community. This "nothing buttery," as Donald MacKay described scientific reductionism, is powerful because it appeals to a truth. Nothing buttery is wrong, however, because it discards the larger truth for only a portion of the truth. It becomes a lie by reducing the truth.

Making Disciples

The mission of the church is to witness to the kingdom by being disciples and making disciples of Jesus Christ. He is the life of the kingdom, the preacher of the kingdom, the embodiment of the kingdom. We live in the kingdom by following him in the power of the Holy Spirit. So discipleship to Jesus Christ is key to our witness to the kingdom. As we follow him we learn to see the kingdom and participate in its work in our world today. As we learn to make disciples, we have to be aware of the obstacles presented by our cultural context. In theological terms, this cultural context is "the world"—all that does not yet acknowledge and submit to Christ's redemptive work.

In the previous section I identified some of the challenges we currently face at the beginning of the twenty-first century. Now I will propose a constructive account of the practice of making disciples in light of those challenges. My aim is to work with an awareness of the challenges so that we have some direction for making disciples within our context but avoid trimming down the practice of making disciples to fit our circumstances.

In modernity, the practice of making disciples must emphasize that in following Jesus Christ we are learning the one way to live that is authentically and truly human. This is the way of freedom and fulfillment for human beings not because it makes us absolutely free to decide who we want to be but because it makes us absolutely free to be what we are created to be. The destiny of human beings is glorious, not because we have so much power and control to determine our destiny but because we are created for glory and by God's grace that glory is ours in Christ.

When we call others to discipleship in Christ in the context of modernity, we must not make the mistake of denying the glory of human beings because modernity has made too much of our status. The mistake of modernity is not to think too highly of human beings but to think that our destiny is under our control. As we become disciples of Jesus Christ, we must do so with the recognition of the high calling that is ours by God's gift to us in creation and redemption.

So the practice of making disciples in the context of modernity involves the call not to give up our freedom but to discover our true freedom in submission to the teacher of the kingdom, the Lord of life, Jesus Christ.

In the context of modernity, the call to discipleship is the call to learn our true destiny from and in Jesus Christ—but also to learn what true human fulfillment is within a world that is in rebellion against its destiny in Christ. That means that following Jesus is a lifelong process of rebellion against the powers of this age. Such lifelong discipline is hard and painful. At some times and in some places it has even been deadly. True discipleship to Christ and life in the kingdom make no sense in the context of modernity and a consumer culture. Certainly the call to discipleship can be trimmed and distorted so that it does make sense in this cultural context. But that so-called good news is a counterfeit gospel and a call to go astray from true discipleship.

True discipleship makes sense in light of the *telos* of the kingdom of God, not in light of the ateleology of modernity. If we try to make sense of it to modernity, then we will betray the good news of Jesus Christ. Why does being a disciple of Jesus teach us to live in the peculiar way that he taught? Because that is what human life is meant to be—in the image used by Jesus, because that's living in accordance with the kingdom of God. Why follow Jesus? Because it is only by faithfully following him that we are brought by God's grace into life. His life, death, and resurrection open up the kingdom to us and the Spirit brings us into that kingdom and into life that is everlasting.

In the context of *postmodernity*, the church may betray the gospel by distorting the things that it needed to emphasize in the context of modernity. In challenging modernity, the church must emphasize that discipleship occurs only in the context of a community of disciples. In challenging postmodernity, the church must maintain this claim about the disciple community but avoid reducing discipleship to this one claim.

In the context of postmodernity, the church may be tempted to abandon the claim that discipleship commits us to a meaningful cosmos that requires our lives to be shaped in one peculiar way that is taught by Jesus Christ and available as a gift. Certainly the disciple community offers precisely that—a community in which to find a home, friendship, companions, and an adventure. But all of that points beyond itself to the *telos* of the cosmos in the kingdom of God in Jesus Christ.

Following Jesus, therefore, is not merely a way of living an interesting life and having an adventure. It is not merely a means of achieving acceptance and membership in a close-knit supportive community. Following Jesus is our participation in the new creation promised and coming into being through the work of Jesus Christ.

In the context of postmodernity, we may be tempted to reduce the making of disciples to initiation into a particular human community that competes for loyalty with other human communities. And so we strive to make the life of the church more attractive and more compelling to those shaped by postmodernity. There is truth in this ambition: we *should* seek to make the community of disciples as attractive as possible. But its attractiveness must always be measured by its commitment to the *telos* of the cosmos—the kingdom of God. The attractiveness of the disciple community must be measured by its conformity to and participation in the life of the kingdom. Then we can, with integrity, call the citizens of postmodernity to the community of disciples.

Also in the context of postmodernity, the question of power must be identified and addressed. Given postmodernity's reduction of human life to the "will to power," the temptation of the call to discipleship is to turn following Jesus into a means to greater power. Remember, in modernity the human quest for power was tied to the conviction that we could acquire control of human destiny through a particular view of science and technology. Postmodernity holds that such optimism about human power as control of destiny is an illusion. So all that remains is the quest for power and control without meaning or purpose beyond a measure of protection and pleasure for our short, meaningless lives.

So the making of disciples of Jesus could easily be turned into an answer to the postmodern quest for power. The appeal of the disciple community is part of this, but so is the call to acquire skills for living through discipleship to Jesus. And as we have been seeing, there is something almost right about the claim that becoming a disciple of Jesus Christ equips us for skillfully making our way in the world. Discipleship is about learning how to live; it is about disciplined life; it is about living in a community that sustains a way of life.

But becoming a disciple of Jesus Christ in the community of disciples is not about acquiring the ability to live life as we choose. Rather, it is about learning to participate in the kingdom, which is the *telos* of the whole cosmos. So the power that we acquire is the power to live according to that reality—the reality climactically revealed in the life, death, and resurrection of Jesus Christ. The power to live this life comes from the Spirit, whose work will be the focus of chapter 10.

Church Discipline

This leads us to a practice of church discipline as the identification of sin in the lives of disciples and the actions taken by the disciple community in response. This area requires great pastoral wisdom among the whole community. Such pastoral wisdom cannot be described or taught in a few words here; it may be acquired only through great effort, participation in the whole range of church practices described here, and eventually by the gift of God (Prov. 2). In order to encourage the practice of church discipline, I will make an argument that identifies why it is so seldom practiced and give some guidance for its renewal.

One of the reasons we have moved away from the practice of discipline is that we have allowed it to be defined by our cultural circumstances instead of by the kingdom of God. In the context of modernity, church discipline is an intrusion into the freedom of individuals to determine their own destiny. If we buy the lie of modernity that human beings can choose their destiny from many options that they themselves can attain, then when we restrict another's freedom or correct their choices, we are working against their flourishing as a person.

In the context of postmodernity, the exercise of discipline seems rooted in the delusion that the cosmos has meaning and purpose. If we buy the lie of postmodernity that human life is a meaningless exercise of power, then we may conclude that we can give no account of the meaningfulness of such discipline except that "it's what we do"—you must conform to belong to our community and have access to its power and protection. In such cases, the discipline of the church merely tells us what we have to do to stay inside the boundaries of the community. But such a practice is not church discipline that makes disciples of Jesus Christ; it is malpractice that directs people to external goods that may be available through membership in the church as a social club. And when those external goods are no longer available in the church or become more easily and readily available elsewhere, the church no longer has significant cultural power.

This last eventuality is precisely what is happening in many communities across North America. For many decades, participation in church (or at a minimum, church attendance) was a means of learning how to behave in society—becoming nice and polite. Beyond this, it provided social connections for economic and political relationships. But when these goods became less important or easier to obtain elsewhere, such as in a civic club or on a soccer bleacher, the church lost social status and attendance fell. These losses are not necessarily bad; they may provide the church in North America with an opportunity to recover its true life in the kingdom.

To embrace the discipline that helps us recover true life in the kingdom, we must overturn the way that we think about discipline—and discipleship—in the church. Consider for a moment the practice of discipline in other settings. When a basketball coach calls timeout to correct the defensive alignment of her team or chew them out for not moving on offense, we do not think that she is doing a bad thing. On the contrary, we admire her insight and tenacity, because the coach and her team have mutually committed themselves to achieving excellence in the practice of basketball. Likewise, when a choral conductor halts practice to correct misread notes or single out one section of voices for special attention, we admire his perceptiveness and his teaching skills, because the conductor and the choir have committed themselves to a *telos*.

These examples of discipline are rather narrow and trivial, but they point us toward a recovery of healthy church discipline. In the church we have committed ourselves to Jesus Christ and the good news of the kingdom of God. These reveal to us the purpose of God's redemptive grace to bring into being a new creation, make us fully human, and glorify God. To participate now in this purpose is a glorious privilege that church discipline enables by identifying when we are not flourishing in the kingdom and directing us back onto the path of flourishing.

In contrast to misconstruals of church discipline that treat it as an enemy of freedom or a meaningless exercise of power, a truly teleological practice of church discipline sees it simply as a part of making disciples who flourish in the kingdom of God. It is helpful to think of the practice as "discipling the brother or sister," but the practice of discipline does go one step beyond the ordinary practice of making disciples.[1] Discipline, as I am considering it here, does not correct simple, immature, or undeveloped life in a disciple; rather, it corrects any deliberate rejection of the teaching of the community or a deliberate abandonment of maturity already achieved by the work of the Holy Spirit.

So church discipline must be understood as the practice by which the disciple community realigns its own life and the life of one or more disciples with the kingdom of God. In this construal, church discipline itself witnesses to the kingdom of God that is our *telos* and participates in that kingdom. It is a practice that makes sense only if we truly believe that life in the kingdom and knowing Jesus Christ constitute the only way of life. Then church discipline becomes an act of compassion, not coercion.

If church discipline is understood in relation to the kingdom of God as our *telos* and as a practice that participates in the life of that kingdom, then the practice of discipline must be characterized by the life of the kingdom in every way. Perhaps the most concise

---

1. See Marlin Jeschke, *Discipling in the Church: Recovering a Ministry of the Gospel* (Scottdale, PA: Herald, 1988). This is a thorough and insightful treatment of church discipline from an Anabaptist perspective that is helpful beyond that tradition. The original edition was published in 1972 as *Discipling the Brother*.

description of this is to say that church discipline must be an exercise of the fruit of the Spirit: loving, joyful, peaceful, patient, kind, good, faithful, gentle, and self-controlled (Gal. 5:22). In this way, the practice of church discipline makes disciples of Jesus Christ who are growing in their participation in the life of the kingdom and in their ability to bear witness to it. This is how human beings flourish.

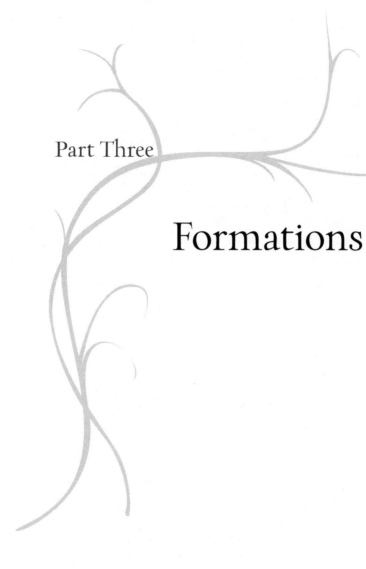

Part Three

Formations

8

Baptism, Eucharist, and Footwashing as Participation in Christic

*I*n the previous two chapters, I have provided a reorientation of the practices of the church in relation to the historical tensions between evangelism and social action and the contemporary cultural tension between modernity and postmodernity. In this and the following chapters, I will provide some accounts of church practices that flesh out the approach that I am advocating. I am keenly aware that my previous chapters have not been as specific as some might hope for in an account of the practices of the church. But such theological work is necessary to the grounding of practices in the actual, concrete life of a community. Unless we recognize and understand the forces in our history and our culture that affect our practices, we run the risk of careless and rash action that may lead to unfaithfulness. Too often practitioners have been unreflective, and theologians have been unconcerned with practices. One of the concerns of this book is to narrow the gap between practice and reflection.

In this chapter, I give an account of three practices of the church that Jesus himself calls us to observe. My intention is to move toward concreteness in the description of these practices. The three practices that I will describe are baptism, Eucharist, and footwashing. The first two are common and accepted practices throughout the church. The third requires some explanation, which I will give when I turn to that practice.

These practices together form the core of the mission of the church to witness to the kingdom and make disciples by teaching Jesus Christ. One of the problems with our observance of them in recent years has been our loss of them as practices. We have seldom understood them and practiced them within a community formed by strong social networks as the embodiment of our conviction about the *telos* of the cosmos. We have not regarded them as a means of strengthening and extending our understanding of the kingdom of God and discipleship to Christ. Moreover, our theological energy has become so focused on our differences about these observances that we have only recently begun to turn our attention to more constructive accounts of what these observances mean for our life as the disciple community. In what follows, I will develop an account of baptism, Eucharist, and footwashing as practices that contribute to the formation of social networks that build up the disciple community, bear witness to the kingdom, and call the world to knowing Christ and participating in his redemptive work. In the end, it is our participation in Christ by means of these practices that forms the church and makes it a witness to the kingdom of God.

Baptism: Dying and Rising with Christ

Baptism is the practice of the church that initiates a life of discipleship. In the church, the New Testament concern for baptism has been obscured because discussions of baptism have so often been consumed by questions about who is baptized, when, how much water is used, and how the observance is related to salvation. In the New Testament, baptism is tied most closely to discipleship.[1] This is true for Jesus and for Paul. In the Great Commission of Matthew's Gospel, the connection between baptism and making disciples is unmistakable: "Then Jesus came to them and said, 'All authority in

---

1. This claim, like many in this chapter, deserves a fuller treatment. I hope to write a future monograph on baptism and discipleship that will argue more fully the position taken here.

heaven and on earth has been given to me. Therefore go and make disciples of all nations, baptizing them in the name of the Father and of the Son and of the Holy Spirit, and teaching them to obey everything I have commanded you. And surely I am with you always, to the very end of the age'" (Matt. 28:18–20 TNIV).

Paul also draws on baptism in his letter to the church in Rome: "We are those who have died to sin; how can we live in it any longer? Or don't you know that all of us who were baptized into Christ Jesus were baptized into his death? We were therefore buried with him through baptism into death in order that, just as Christ was raised from the dead through the glory of the Father, we too may live a new life" (Rom. 6:2–4 TNIV). In this passage Paul ties baptism to discipleship—living a "new life"—and gives us a wonderfully concise account of baptism as a practice by which we die with Christ and are raised with him.

Baptism is the initiating practice of the church because it marks the new life in Christ that characterizes the disciple community. This practice has been a source of distinction and even division in the history of the church. But if we develop an understanding of baptism as a practice, we may begin to form a consensus about its meaning even in the midst of differences.

As a practice, baptism makes sense only in light of the kingdom of God as the *telos* of the cosmos. One of the indispensable meanings of baptism, whatever its mode, is that it is an enactment of our identity with Christ in his death and resurrection to such an extent that it may also be described as our own death and resurrection. Such a description is tenable only if our death is death to one kingdom and our resurrection is to a new kingdom. Paul calls the kingdom to which we die "Sin" and the kingdom to which we rise "Life." Why would anyone allow himself to be "put to death"? Only because he is convinced that the reign into which he was born (see Rom. 5:20) is destined for condemnation and the reign into which he is promised resurrection is "eternal life" (Rom. 6:23).

Romans 6:2–4 also tells us something about the agent of baptism. Paul makes it clear that the death and resurrection enacted in baptism are the work of God. We cannot kill ourselves in such a way that we identify with Christ, nor can we raise ourselves to new life in Christ. That work is possible only by the power of God. Yet it is the church that is commissioned to baptize. So we may see that the agent in the practice of baptism is God, who delegates authority to the church, so that the disciple community acts as God's agent in baptism. This understanding of agency teaches us something fundamental about the making of disciples: That work is entirely dependent on God's act in Jesus Christ and the continuing presence of God's power through the Holy Spirit in the world. But the church is commissioned to witness to that work and to make disciples.

This understanding of the agency of the church in baptism may help us rethink one of the thorny differences on baptism. If we understand that the primary agent of baptism is God and the church is delegated as God's agent, then we need to give more attention to baptism as an act—a practice—of the disciple community. Thus, it is more important and foundational to ask about the community that is baptizing than to ask about the age or responsibility of the person being baptized. When we ask about the self-understanding of the "baptismal community" as a *disciple community*, few parts of the church do very well. Neither those communities that baptize infants nor those that baptize "believers" are very fruitful as a disciple community for the baptized.[2]

The issue is not the age of the person being baptized, nor is it the priority of conscious faith; rather, the question is, are those being baptized being initiated into a community that understands itself as a community of discipleship and takes responsibility for the training of the new disciples? When baptism is framed as a practice tied to the making of disciples who live in and bear witness to the kingdom, both infant baptizers and non–infant baptizers face the same questions. Do we have practices of discipleship into which this person is being initiated? Does our practice of baptism itself reflect its place as the initial act of discipling another?

So we seek to understand baptism as a practice that initiates us in discipleship by teaching that God is the agent working through the disciple community. It teaches us that discipleship is not the achievement of human effort but the gift of new life in Christ. It teaches

2. One common way of contrasting these communities is to talk about infant and adult baptism. Such language is misleading, however, because some communities that reject "infant" baptism do baptize young children if they can give a satisfactory account of their understanding of the gospel and their own faith.

us that our new life is available only in the disciple community, to whom and through whom God gives the Holy Spirit. Thus, the life of the community and the life of the disciple are directed beyond themselves to God and the kingdom in which we participate with God. And this entire account merely unfolds the reason for baptism in the name of the Father, Son, and Holy Spirit (Matt. 28:19). The Father is the font of our life, the Son is the form of our life, and the Spirit is the power of our life in the kingdom.

In the church, this understanding of the practice of baptism must be made concrete. One way of making baptismal practice conform to this account is to make baptism a central event in the life of the church. Some communities make baptism central in the space and time of their life together, but too many do not. For many churches today, baptism no longer occurs in the place where most of the community life occurs. It is often moved to the spatial periphery of community life—to a baptistery borrowed briefly from another church, a swimming pool in someone's backyard, or a public space such as a beach. These may at first appear to be admirable claims upon all space as God's. But when we understand baptism as the initiating event for life in the disciple community, we should recognize the necessity of locating the event at the spatial center of community life. Many communities, then, need to make a more concerted effort to make the practice of baptism spatially central. This does not mean that every church must have a worship space with a baptistery, but it does mean that creative solutions need to be developed.

In addition to being central in ecclesial space, baptism should be central in ecclesial time. In some segments of the church tradition, baptism takes place at the high points of the liturgical year, especially Advent and Easter. But in many North American churches today, baptism has been moved not only away from these central moments but even outside the regular time of the community's gathering. In these communities baptism occurs not when the church is regularly gathered but at an "optional" time in an afternoon or evening. In the context of this kind of malpractice, we should not be surprised that baptism itself appears optional, as does the discipleship that it is supposed to initiate. For baptism to be sustained or renewed as a church practice, it must be central to the community's time.

It should be integrated into the regular life of the community and placed at the high points of the community's life.

Baptism must be brought to the center not only of the disciple community's space and time but also of its teaching. The practice of baptism, as I have too briefly argued, embodies the gospel as the call to discipleship—new life in Christ made possible by God's work. Baptism teaches us that we do not have this new life by our own power. It teaches us that discipleship is a new way of life that breaks decisively, on a cosmic scale, with our old life. It teaches us that we live that life only in the disciple community. Baptism teaches us that life in the kingdom is death to the old and life in the new that is Jesus Christ. These convictions should move us to intentionally bring baptism into the center of the church's teaching.

In some settings, this will mean an extensive program of instruction in discipleship as part of the practice of baptism before the actual baptism. This is being recovered in some communities through the renewal of catechesis. In other settings it may mean an extensive program of discipleship that follows baptism but is an integral part of it, not an option. In communities that continue to baptize infants as initiation into the disciple community, there must be a program by which each baptism leads not only to confirmation of faith but also growth and continuation in discipleship. In all settings, baptism that is central in space and time can also become a moment for all members of the disciple community to remember their baptism and to teach the meaning of baptism as a practice of the community that witnesses to the *telos* of the cosmos.

This last emphasis may be further understood and exemplified by the involvement of the social network of the community in baptism. While the significance of godparents has been severely compromised in most communities that recognize them, the meaning of baptism as a practice may be renewed through the social relationships essential to discipleship subsequent to the initiating act of baptism. This will take different forms in different communities. In some the true significance of godparents as disciplers may be recovered. In other communities a small group or class or other group of people committing themselves to accountability in discipleship may be involved in the baptism either in the preparation before or in follow-up after. The necessity of community may also be made clear at the time of baptism by having others reflect publicly on their baptisms and their continued growth in understanding its significance for the life of discipleship. But this involvement must not be casual or unexplained, as if it were enough just to do it. The practice must be interpreted and its significance explained. The pastor as language teacher becomes very important in making the practice of baptism central to the teaching of the church.

Lord's Supper: Eating and Drinking with Jesus

Earlier I spoke of this observance as "Eucharist." Here I have labeled it "Lord's Supper." Others would call it Communion. This variation exemplifies the first problem with an account of this practice—the divisions within the church over its understanding. In baptism, the church has at least held on to a common vocabulary even as differences of understanding have developed. The same cannot be said of "the meal Jesus gave us."[3] Here the differences are enshrined in vocabulary. As I explore this observance as a practice, I hope to identity some ways that we may recognize something common even across the differences.

If baptism can be identified as the initiating practice of the church, the Lord's Supper may be called its sustaining practice. This phrase could easily be misunderstood as advocacy for a particular historic position amid the controversy over the meaning of the Lord's Supper. But when I call this the sustaining practice of the church, I mean that as a claim about the practice no matter which historic position one takes. To claim that the Lord's Supper is the sustaining practice of the church is to say that it is the ongoing practice of the community that enables us to participate (through memory, real presence, con- or trans-substantiation) in God's continual provision of new life for God's people.

The Lord's Supper incorporates us into the life of the kingdom by the act of remembering Christ as the One who teaches and embodies the kingdom. We cannot participate in the life of the kingdom

---

3. This quote is the delightful title of the pithy book by Tom Wright, *The Meal Jesus Gave Us: Understanding Holy Communion* (Louisville, KY: Westminster John Knox, 2002).

without knowing what that life looks like. Remembering Jesus's whole way of life, his death, and his resurrection in the Lord's Supper teaches us that *telos*. In this celebration of a meal, we should recall Jesus's own table fellowship with those on the margins and those at the center. We should remember that he celebrated it in the company of one who would betray him and many who would abandon him.

The Eucharist also teaches us the kingdom by calling us into the recognition that we are at the table by God's invitation on the basis of the work of Christ. Once again, we learn that we live toward the *telos* of the cosmos, not the work of our own power and control but the gift of God. We celebrate this meal as a witness to the kingdom and its work in our world. And so as we practice the Lord's Supper, we grow into the life of the kingdom.

Some of the present life of the kingdom is well represented in the practice of the Eucharist. Most communities witness clearly to Christ's work as the foundation and core of the celebration. Where the practice of the Eucharist could be strengthened often is in the way that it participates in and develops the social network that constitutes the church.

In order to make Communion a practice that strengthens the social fabric of the church, we need to recover a realistic sense of it as a communal meal without losing the centrality of the work of Christ as its foundation. When we eat with one another, we are participating in an activity that sustains all our lives. None of us can live without this ongoing provision. We learn the same in Communion. We are together in our dependence upon God. If we are to be truthful in our gathering, then we must also be reconciled to one another. This requires practices of confession and forgiveness toward one another. Imagine what could happen if we challenged participants to maturity as disciples of Jesus Christ by being reconciled to one another as part of the practice of Communion. That such a suggestion strikes fear in many of us and seems an absurdly unobtainable goal reveals a lack of maturity and a lack of understanding of the way of discipleship in our churches.

But if we believe that such a practice is indeed one embodiment of our *telos* and witness to the kingdom, then what steps might we plan to bring communities of disciples to such a practice and the sacrifice it entails? Is it not striking that even as we celebrate the sacrifice of Jesus Christ that makes our new life possible, we shrink back from any practice that might call for sacrifice on our part? This sacrificial practice makes sense only if the kingdom of God in Christ is indeed the *telos* of the cosmos. But because the kingdom *is* come in Jesus Christ, we should embrace joyfully the practice of that kingdom that we are taught in Communion.

In addition to the practice of reconciliation, Communion teaches us the nature of God's hospitality.[4] This hospitality needs to be practiced in significant and intentional ways in connection with the Lord's Supper. One way to do this is to occasionally precede or follow the celebration with a meal together. This meal could take place communally in one setting, or it could be held in many homes before or after the communal celebration of the Eucharist. Another way would be to regularly follow Communion with serving a meal at a community kitchen or homeless shelter. The way God feeds us at the table could be acted out communally by occasionally bringing gifts for a food bank as part of the service. In many churches one regular part of the celebration of Communion is an offering for the church's benevolent fund. Although I have been in many churches where this takes place, I have yet to hear any explicit connection made between the offering and the Lord's Supper. A significant teaching moment is lost when we do not think carefully about this observance as a practice.

Within the Christian community, we may recover and build something of the social network that sustains practices by modifying the way we provide and prepare Communion. In our culture, the provision and preparation of Communion are often impersonal commercial transactions: someone goes to the local grocery store and purchases the necessary goods. What if a congregation occasionally adopted a thicker, communal practice of preparation? For example, imagine assigning preparation to a youth group, Bible study, or small group, who would then plan how to provide the "meal." Perhaps

---

4. I explore this in Jonathan R. Wilson, *Gospel Virtues: Practicing Faith, Hope, and Love in Uncertain Times* (Downers Grove, IL: InterVarsity Press, 1998), chap. 8. Among several book-length treatments of Christian hospitality, one of the best is Christine Pohl, *Making Room: Recovering Hospitality in the Christian Tradition* (Grand Rapids: Eerdmans, 1999).

they would meet in the church kitchen on Saturday for a lesson in baking bread. They might produce many more loaves than necessary for the Eucharist and take them to those who are in need, announcing where the bread has come from and why it is being provided. Or a similar program might be incorporated into a children's Sunday school program, with two weeks of teaching and acting out the exodus story followed by well-planned, closely supervised baking of unleavened bread that the children then bring into the sanctuary for Eucharist. Similar possibilities may be imagined for the provision of wine—with obvious complexities for some traditions!

When we do think about the Lord's Supper as a practice, we can see many different ways that it may become a means of learning more clearly what it means to participate in the kingdom of God as the *telos* of the cosmos. We learn that our new life in that kingdom depends upon God's provision for us. We remember that the life of that kingdom begins in the sacrifice required when Jesus embodied the kingdom in this rebellious world. We see that the life of that kingdom cannot be conquered by death as we live out the powerful presence of the Spirit in confessing, forgiving, and being reconciled. We witness to the kingdom when we extend hospitality and serve others.

Footwashing: Stooping and Serving with Jesus

Although footwashing is a much-neglected observance, it should be a central practice of the disciple community. As it happens, I grew up in a tradition that regarded footwashing as one of three ordinances of the church, along with baptism and Communion.[5] I will not here argue for its inclusion as an ordinance or sacrament, but I do suggest that it be recognized and established as a practice of the church. I am encouraged in this suggestion by many younger members of the church who are deeply moved by the experience of footwashing but lack a theological framework for its practice. I am also encouraged by casual remarks from other theologians in support of a wider practice of footwashing.

5. See J. Matthew Pinson, *The Washing of the Saints' Feet* (Nashville: Randall House Publications, 2006).

Some churches incorporate a ritual of footwashing in their Maundy Thursday service (the evening before Good Friday). Others may incorporate it into services installing leaders of a congregation or some wider body of disciples. These are good, but if we think about observances of the church that participate in kingdom life, form us as disciples, and bear witness to the world, it makes sense that footwashing should be a regular practice of the disciple community.

John's Gospel provides the only account of Jesus washing the disciples' feet:

> It was just before the Passover Festival. Jesus knew that the hour had come for him to leave this world and go to the Father. Having loved his own who were in the world, he loved them to the end.
>
> The evening meal was in progress, and the devil had already prompted Judas, the son of Simon Iscariot, to betray Jesus. Jesus knew that the Father had put all things under his power, and that he had come from God and was returning to God; so he got up from the meal, took off his outer clothing, and wrapped a towel around his waist. After that, he poured water into a basin and began to wash his disciples' feet, drying them with the towel that was wrapped around him. . . .
>
> When he had finished washing their feet, he put on his clothes and returned to his place. "Do you understand what I have done for you?" he asked them. "You call me 'Teacher' and 'Lord,' and rightly so, for that is what I am. Now that I, your Lord and Teacher, have washed your feet, you also should wash one another's feet. I have set you an example that you should do as I have done for you. Very truly I tell you, servants are not greater than their master, nor are messengers greater than the one who sent them. Now that you know these things, you will be blessed if you do them." (John 13:1–5, 12–17 TNIV)

Some argue that we have rightly dispensed with footwashing because it was a broader cultural practice of Jesus's day that we no longer observe. However, this passage and the observance of footwashing are so rich for making disciples and learning to live in the kingdom that we should urgently seek to renew its practice.

In the passage from John, Jesus's actions are explicitly tied to his own understanding of the *telos* of the cosmos and his place in it. His washing the disciples' feet makes sense only as life in the kingdom. Notice that he does not deny his status: he is Teacher and Lord. But in the kingdom, Teacher and Lord mean servant. This teaches us that as disciples empowered for new life in Christ by the Spirit, we do have status and a glorious destiny. At the same time, in God's kingdom our status and our destiny are the basis for serving others. And that service must take its direction from the life of the kingdom, not the life of the world. We are not present in the world and others' lives in order to make their worldly dreams come true. We are there as witnesses to the kingdom.

So the practice of footwashing brings us to stoop, not because we are weak but because God has made us strong, and the strength that we have been given is a means of service. If baptism is the initiating practice of the disciple community, and Eucharist is our sustaining practice, footwashing is our guiding practice. It teaches us to take all that we have been given by God in Christ through the Holy Spirit and serve the world as an act of witness to the kingdom.

In this understanding, the first step for the disciple community is to figure out how to incorporate the practice of footwashing appropriately in its communal life. In the church where I grew up, men and women gathered in separate rooms to wash one another's feet. At Westmont College, where I taught for many years, the student government annually sponsored a chapel service that centered on footwashing. It took place in the school gymnasium, a very lively public setting, and was practiced among a whole range of people—students, faculty, and staff. What is appropriate will vary among communities.

Once the basic setting is agreed, the community must work out ways in which the observance becomes a practice. How much teaching is needed? Who will do it? In what setting? Should it be done in weeks leading up to the observance? What governing and guiding structures of the church must participate in this process? But the most important questions have to do with how this observance is situated in the social network of the community so that the community is strengthened, disciples grow, and the kingdom is displayed and understood more fully. Some of this can be accomplished through the teaching that introduces and follows the practice. But it needs to be extended by additional practices that follow from footwashing and carry the community further into the life of the kingdom. Are there additional ways of serving that might carry the practice of footwashing into the disciple community and beyond? What if the observance of footwashing is followed by an afternoon of service to others in which every church member is urged to participate? What if that service is done out of joy for what Jesus Christ did when he laid aside his outer garments to serve his disciples? What if we ask ourselves whether the service we are planning to perform will require us to take off our good clothes and get down and dirty? Then we are beginning to learn life in the kingdom as we follow Jesus Christ, our Teacher and Lord.

Conclusion

My aim in this chapter has been not to present a highly condensed but comprehensive account of these observances of the church but rather to focus narrowly on their observance *as practices*. Even so, my account does not attempt to say everything that might be said about baptism, Eucharist, and footwashing as practices. But I have given some direction for thinking about them as practices. These practices enable us to participate in Christ as his body. They anticipate the fullness of the kingdom, when we are made new in every way, when we are reconciled fully to one another and to God, and when all that we are becomes a means of loving service to one another. By participating in Christ through them, we continually learn more about the kingdom in which life is given to us.

The real work of thinking this out further must take place within the actual life of disciple communities that have caught a vision for life in the kingdom, becoming disciples of Jesus, and the practices that participate in and extend that vision as a witness to the world of God's redemptive holiness and love.

9

Confession as the Shape of the Church

*I*n the creeds confessed by most traditions, we confess "one holy, catholic, apostolic church." This confession may be troubling to many because it seems to require a deliberate ignorance of the actual church that we have. At times it may seem to require a level of willful denial that is almost comic in its absurdity. Who could confess with a straight face that the church is one, holy, catholic, and apostolic?

In this chapter, I give just such an account of the church not only with a straight face but also with great joy, because I too have been troubled for years by this confession and have over those years arrived at accommodations that enabled me to make the confession. But such accommodations eventually became uncomfortable and unlivable. Then in the context of developing the argument of this book, I confronted the necessity of broadening my account of the life of the church in its practices to include an account of the doctrinal tradition of the church. As I struggled with that challenge, I began to see how my own struggle to confess the church as one, holy, catholic, and apostolic could be resolved by an account of the practices of the church in light of our participation in the kingdom of God as the *telos* of the cosmos. This account does not solve or dissolve the questions, but it does resolve them so that we can see why the confession makes sense, and it even accounts for the tension that we rightly perceive in our confession.

Before turning to that account, I must emphasize the importance of this chapter as a signal that this book is not satisfactory as a *comprehensive* ecclesiology, though I do claim that it is a work in ecclesiology. This assertion requires some explanation. Often the theological tradition of the church develops expectations in a particular historical stream of what the treatment of some locus of doctrine will look like. How will it be organized? What topics must be covered? Which controversies and debates must be addressed and resolved? This book fits very few expectations for an ecclesiology, as a quick comparison with any recent work of ecclesiology will reveal. Moreover, it takes practices as its organizing concept. Surely that removes it from the realm of doctrine and systematic theology and places it in the field of practical theology.

If I accepted the standard expectations, then the descriptions of the previous paragraph would stand. But this work is itself an expression of my desire to erase the distinctions between the fields of theology. My view is that the divisions of theology are largely rooted in an unfortunate attempt to justify the continuation of theological study during the rise of the German research university. This claim is controversial, and I cannot defend it here. Nevertheless, this book stands as a contribution to erasing the divisions among types of theological works, regardless of their origin.

This brief excursus on the relationship between my approach here and the doctrinal tradition of the church explains the slightly different character of this chapter. In previous chapters I maintained a consistent and clear focus on practices in which doctrine is present but subsumed in the account of practices. In this chapter, I maintain a consistent and clear focus on doctrine, with practices providing a resolution to the doctrinal conundrums that we often identify in ecclesiology. I will argue that when we confess that the church is one, holy, catholic, and apostolic, we confess its relationship to the kingdom of God and its participation in the life of that kingdom.

One

It is exceedingly troubling to confess belief in the unity of the church in the presence of so many apparent divisions and in a world where many days we hear news of Christians killing other Christians. To overcome this dissonance, the church employs a range of assertions. When confronted with Christians killing Christians, we often claim with some justification that the antagonists are "Christian in name only." When confronted with historic divisions among traditions, recourse is often made to the invisible, true church. These strategies seek to assert the present unity of the church in the midst of apparent disunity by claiming that the one true church is already united even now, though invisibly. In the past decades, many devoted significant time and energy to achieving the visible unity of the church.[1]

Both of these approaches to the confession of the church's oneness are complex and nuanced. I will not try to survey or critique the range of discussions and positions. Rather, in what follows I will offer another way of looking at and for the unity of the church.

When we confess the oneness of the church, we assert our conviction that God gathers one people and commissions one people to bear witness to God's kingdom. The oneness of the church is not simply a claim about the church; it is ultimately a claim about the kingdom of God and the way God has determined for that kingdom to be made known to the world. It is this one people, the church, through whom the kingdom is made known. (As I argued in chapter 7, that does not mean that the kingdom is present only in the church; the kingdom is greater than the church and is at work outside the church. But it is in the church that the work of that kingdom is learned and pointed out.) So the oneness of the church is its unity in witness to only one thing—the kingdom of God—and its oneness as the only people through whom God has chosen that witness should be carried out.

This understanding of the oneness of the church teaches us that the many apparent divisions in the church may be celebrated not by making them all the same but by recognizing that they all bear witness to the one reality of the kingdom of God. Of course they do so imperfectly; that is a topic we will turn to in

1. A recent and very helpful approach is Carl E. Braaten and Robert W. Jenson, eds., *In One Body through the Cross: The Princeton Proposal for Christian Unity* (Grand Rapids: Eerdmans, 2003).

the next section of this chapter. Here we must recognize that we will resolve the differences among the churches not by relating the differences directly to one another but by relating them first to the kingdom.

Take, for example, baptism. The disunity of the church on baptism is problematic when the various practices are compared to one another. But when they are compared to the kingdom, they begin to be resolved. This resolution does not occur immediately or without effort. And we discover along the way that our churches understand the relationship between baptism and the kingdom with different emphases. But when we begin to identity these and relate them properly to the kingdom, we can begin to see that our practices are all directed toward the same *telos*. At this point, we may be able to find ways to accept and incorporate one another's practices on our own bases.

For instance, imagine what might happen if proponents of both infant baptism and believer baptism had to articulate how their practice of baptism relates to the kingdom of God. (I made some suggestions about this in chapter 8.) As they sought to describe this relationship, their own understanding might be modified, but more important, both views would find common ground in the attempt to bear witness to the kingdom and incorporate others into it. From this common ground, both views might find something of significance in the other—perhaps an insight into the nature of the kingdom and life in it that their own practice had not shown them. In such a case, the proponents of one practice might seek to enrich their own tradition with insights from the other. At the very least, proponents of both views might be able to identify what is commendable in the other and why they should recognize one another as participants in the same *telos*.

The understanding of the unity of the church in relation to the kingdom that I am advocating also clarifies the tension between the church's visibility and its invisibility. When we restrict the confession of oneness strictly to the church (apart from its relationship to the kingdom), we have little choice but to appeal to the invisibility of the one true church. But when we acknowledge that the unity of the church is its relationship to the kingdom, we have a different resolution at hand.

In the context of the church's oneness in relation to the kingdom, we must learn that our lack of visible unity in itself bears witness to the good news that God's work of redemption is larger than the church—it includes all of creation. The lack of full visible unity in the church also bears witness to the "not yet" of the kingdom. The kingdom that is God's full redemption of the cosmos is present and at work in this age, but it is not yet fully present in creation. The incompleteness of the church's unity is a necessary reminder of the redemption for which we wait. So in our confession of oneness we do not appeal to the invisible true church; instead we witness to the larger and still coming kingdom of God.

This witness, however, does not excuse us from working toward unity as the church before the watching world. Indeed, the call to witness makes even more urgent the task of articulating our unity. We fail in our witness when the world hears from the church our attempts to differentiate ourselves from one another in our efforts to bring seeking persons into our community. Instead, what the world should be hearing from us is how our various practices bear witness to the one work of redemption in Christ. The focus should not be on differentiating ourselves from one another to establish competitive advantage and increase market share. How utterly we betray the kingdom and bring judgment on ourselves when we do such things. Rather, our focus should be on joyful celebration of the many ways that we can bear witness to the kingdom and its richness.

So the one church is found in the source of our life, the mission we are given, the destiny toward which we live, and the God whom we serve. Is this not what Paul meant: "There is one body and one Spirit, just as you were called to the one hope of your calling, one Lord, one faith, one baptism, one God and Father of all, who is above all and through all and in all" (Eph. 4:4–6)? We do not discover the oneness of the church, then, by directing our gaze toward the church and somehow making it look like one thing. Rather, the oneness of the church is revealed as we direct all of our diversity toward seeing the one work of God, the redemption of creation through Jesus Christ, which is God's kingdom.[2]

2. This work of oneness is helped by the kind of analysis, argument, and direction that I give here and that others give elsewhere. But it depends penultimately on the gifts and

120

Holy

To confess the holiness of the church seems, if possible, more absurd and even more offensive than confessing the unity of the church.[3] In the wake of historical offenses such as the Crusades and slavery and contemporary scandals, the church appears to be anything but holy. Indeed, one can imagine that confessing the church's holiness could, if done wrongly, make situations even worse by leading to self-righteousness and denial of wrongdoing. Such denial, in the name of being faithful to the confession of a holy church, could excuse, cover up, and perpetuate the unholy behavior of the church.

In the cause of trying to moderate and even end some of the injustice perpetrated by the church, I am tempted to argue for dispensing with the claim that the church is holy. Such an argument, if accepted, would certainly remove a difficult theological problem for the church. Or would it? Would we actually gain anything by abandoning this confession, or would the abuses continue because, after all, we are not holy? In reality, nothing would be gained by abandoning the confession of the church's holiness—but we would lose something critical to the good news of God's redemption of the cosmos in Jesus Christ.

The confession that the church is holy is a confession about the church's relationship to the *telos* of the cosmos. To assert that the church is holy is to testify to its present participation and its future completion in the kingdom of God.[4] When we think of holiness, what generally comes to mind is purity. Yet purity, while essential,

---

character of leaders in the church who work for the kind of unity described here. Sadly, the church often lacks such leaders. I explore this problem in an as yet unpublished essay, "Virtues on the Boundaries, Virtues at the Center," presented to the Evangelical Ethics Interest Group at the 2004 annual meeting of the Society of Christian Ethics.

3. There are some good things to learn about the holiness of the church in John Webster, *Holiness* (Grand Rapids: Eerdmans, 2003), chap. 3. The outline of my exposition was in place before I read Webster's treatment. There are many places where our accounts coincide or complement one another. But there are also some differences that I will note along the way.

4. At several points in his chapter on the holiness of the church, Webster opposes the language of participation in God as a description of the church's life. I am not convinced by his arguments, but I am also not using *participation* in the way to which he objects: I refer it to the kingdom of God, not to ontological participation in God.

121

is only one aspect of holiness. Holiness is the conviction that the church's life depends upon its participation in the kingdom of God by the initiating and continuing work of God. The church is holy by virtue of its origin and its destiny.

The church originates in the choice of God to call a people to serve God by bearing witness of the kingdom. In Ephesians and in much of the history of the church, this choice is called "election." This election is rooted not in our worthiness or goodness or power but purely in God's choice of a people to bring glory to God by being made God's people. So election is not a claim to privilege or power, except as that privilege means bearing witness and that power is for serving.[5]

This being chosen and called and commissioned by God is the holiness, the "set-apartness," of the church in its origin. If we abandoned the confession of the church as holy, then we would be losing this confession that the church owes its existence, its mission, and its empowerment to God, not to any human agency. The loss of that claim would set the church adrift, with nothing to anchor it or to guide it through history. Even though the church often fails to practice the confession of holiness by claiming to live by its own power or refusing to bring its sin before God in confession, the confession of the holiness of the church must be sustained. Only by such persistent practice will the church have, within its own life, the claim that calls forth prophets who speak on God's behalf to God's people.

This reference to the prophets takes us one more step along in understanding the holiness of the church as our participation in the kingdom of God. The church is holy by its origin in the life of the kingdom by God's election. But in that kingdom the church is not immune from judgment and discipline. Indeed, just as God's people of the Old Testament suffered severe judgment that purged, refined, and restored them to God's purposes, so the people of the New Testament face the same redemptive discipline for unfaithfulness. To be set apart for witness to the kingdom means that we also become the place where the purifying fire of God's grace is made known.

5. This is a powerful theme in the indispensable work of Lesslie Newbigin. For a concise guide to the significance of this theme for Newbigin, see George R. Hunsberger, *Bearing the Witness of the Spirit: Lesslie Newbigin's Theology of Cultural Plurality* (Grand Rapids: Eerdmans, 1998), chap. 2.

In addition to claiming the church's origin in God's gracious choice, the confession of the church's holiness points toward our destiny. The kingdom in which we live and toward which we journey is the holy kingdom of life. This kingdom is the one *telos* of the cosmos. If we do not participate in its life, its holiness, then we have no part in it. And its holiness is not partial or incomplete; no, the holiness of the kingdom is the fullness of life. Here a few words about "holiness" and "life" are necessary.

We tend to think of "holiness" and "life" as two separate things. In casual conversation we can use these words to refer to different things. But at a more reflective level, we see that the two are identical. This does not mean that our holy life as human beings is identical to God's life of holiness. But it does mean that "the holiness of God" simply is God's life, and "the holiness of humanity" simply is human life. In other words, if we truly believe that the kingdom of God is the one and only *telos* of the cosmos, then we are not free to choose between "holy living" and "unholy living." Holiness is living, and it is, in the most profound way, the only path of life. Unholiness is dying, and it is, in the most profound way, the path to death.

So to confess the holiness of the church is to confess that the church's destiny is life, not death, by virtue of our being lined up rightly with the kingdom of God. This lining up rightly in the work of God as our origin in God's gracious choice is completed in God's gracious purpose. It is what scripture means by *righteousness* and *justification*, but those words have become so burdened by misunderstandings that I use the imagery above to try to communicate the glorious future of God's promise. This means then that the holiness of the church in the kingdom is the fulfillment of God's plan for creation. It is what God intends for this world to be.[6]

By the church's confession of the certainty of holiness in God's gracious election and consummation, it sets before the world the

---

6. Because this holiness is the fulfillment of the *telos* of the cosmos, it is dangerously misleading to say that "the Church's holiness is therefore an *alien* sanctity" (Webster, *Holiness*, 62, his italics). Webster's "therefore" refers back to his assertion that the holiness of the church is grounded in the work of God. This helps, but the language of "alien" makes it seem, wrongly, that God's work is to make us something other than human—in other words, that holiness is alien to our humanity. Holiness is God's work, but it is God's work that makes us human, fully human, properly human, in fulfillment of our *telos*.

good news of God's redemption. Without this confession of holiness, the news of the kingdom is no longer good. The promise that God sustains life forever in the fulfillment of God's kingdom is made to the cosmos. So the proper confession of the church's holiness is not our prideful assertion of being better than others or being more lovable or worthy of God's praise. Rather, the church is holy because the kingdom in which we have our origin and destiny is the kingdom of life. And we are called by God to bear witness to that kingdom.

Catholic

The immediate problem in some settings with confessing the catholicity of the church is that many think that *catholic* refers to the Roman Catholic Church. But in the creeds and the larger theological tradition, the term *catholic* is used in the sense of "universal." Even in those settings where *catholic* is understood to refer to the breadth of the church, in some sense its "universality," the word can carry resonances that make it distracting. So in many congregations, the term *universal* substitutes for *catholic* in the creeds. However, I will use *catholic* here because no other term quite conveys all its color. *Universal* has the rather innocuous and limited sense of breadth in space and time. *Catholic* claims that sort of breadth but also connotes an embrace of variety and style that is crucial to understanding one aspect of the church's participation in and witness to the kingdom. So I will use *catholic* throughout this section as I develop its meaning and trust that even its strangeness will be a means of learning something crucial about the church's life in the kingdom.

To confess the catholicity of the church is to confess that the people of God bear witness to a kingdom whose human inhabitants are not from one people, one race, one sex, one language but are "members of every tribe and language and people and nation" (Rev. 5:9 TNIV). The catholicity of the church is one sign of the church's life in that kingdom. Catholicity is not a survival strategy or marketing ploy or aesthetic expression; it is the reality of the kingdom in the life of the church.

Catholicity was one of the earliest and persistent problems of members of the early church as they sought to understand the question of identity and cultural practices in this new people, this one new humanity that God was creating in and through Jesus Christ (Eph. 2). Would this church be Jewish? Would it be Gentile? Would it be two—one Jew, one Gentile? At this point the questions begin to draw in the question of unity as well as catholicity. But the question of catholicity helps us bring a focus that is different. The question of catholicity is this: given that the church is one, what will that one church look like in its identity, its culture, its practices, its language, its national loyalty? The answer is summarized in the term *catholic*.

The catholicity of the church recognizes that no one culture has been given by God for the life of the kingdom. Or to put it positively, catholicity bears witness to the openness of every culture to God's redemptive work, which converts culture to a means of living in the kingdom.[7] The kingdom is not the privileging of one segment of humanity; it is the *telos* of all creation. So for the church to participate in the life of the kingdom and bear witness to it, the church must be catholic.

Catholicity presents a different kind of problem from unity and holiness. For the latter two, the problem is the dissonance between the confession and appearance. For catholicity, the problems are more practical. Which cultural practices are redeemed or redeemable? Is our objection to something merely a matter of cultural difference or familiarity, or is it an identification of something that cannot be redeemed and brought into the kingdom?

One way to think about catholicity is to regard it as hospitality extended to family members who are strangers. This is an issue that the early church struggled with early on and consistently as Jews and Gentiles struggled to become "catholic" and extend hospitality to one another. The earliest church council, at Jerusalem (Acts 15), was devoted to this very question and understood that the nature of the gospel, the character of the kingdom, was at stake.

---

7. The brilliant insights of Lamin Sanneh display this understanding of catholicity in many of his books, especially *Translating the Message* (Maryknoll, NY: Orbis, 1989), and *Whose Religion Is Christianity? The Gospel beyond the West* (Grand Rapids: Eerdmans, 2003).

Were eating pork and practicing circumcision matters to be left to particular cultures and welcomed into the life of the church as witness to the kingdom? Or were they offenses to kingdom life that had to be excluded? What about eating meat offered to idols or the sexual practices of the Gentiles? After "much debate" (Acts 15:7), the council moved to a decision guided by the gifts of its leaders and the Holy Spirit. They embraced the first two but excluded the last two. Note that they do not tell Jews that they must cease the practice of circumcision, nor do they tell the Gentiles to begin the practice. They do not create one culture out of the two but create a catholicity that welcomes both in line with the life of the kingdom of God.

This welcoming catholicity was not learned with ease. Even after the Jerusalem Council, Paul's letters regularly and extensively address the question of catholicity, especially in relation to circumcision and table fellowship. Questions of catholicity continue to confront the church. If the church had one language and one culture to enforce on all disciples, the questions would be less persistent and less difficult to answer. But because the church lives in the kingdom that itself embraces the cosmos in God's redemptive purpose, the church must faithfully struggle with the continuing questions.

In this struggle the church draws on many resources that are reflected in Acts 15: the broad cultural experiences of disciples (Peter and Paul's experience of faith among the Gentiles), the gifts scattered among the church by the Holy Spirit (the various contributions of the gathered leaders), the teaching of scripture (James's quotation of the Old Testament, Acts 15:16–18), and the guidance of the Holy Spirit. In our struggle to discern, we must keep in view that although much can be redeemed, not everything belongs in the life of the church as witness to the kingdom. The early church excluded a number of things from the surrounding culture (the sacrificial system of Israel, the sexual practices of the Greeks). In John's vision of the new Jerusalem, he sees that

> the nations will walk by its light, and the kings of the earth will bring their glory into it. Its gates will never be shut by day—and there will be no night there. People will bring into it the glory and the honor of the nations. But nothing unclean will enter it, nor anyone who

practices abomination or falsehood, but only those who are written in the Lamb's book of life. (Rev. 21:24–27)

This is a vision of the *telos* of the cosmos in the kingdom of God to which the church bears witness by its catholicity, embracing all from everywhere that participates in the redemptive work of God.

The practice of catholicity is especially important and accessible today because of the ease of travel and communication among cultures. But it is even more important and accessible because of the modern missionary movement and the rise of worldwide Christianity. For the first time in history, more disciples of Jesus Christ live south of the equator than north.[8] The practice of catholicity is today truer than ever to the life of the church and the already of the kingdom. And it is more within our reach: as most of our communities become more diverse, our congregations can become more catholic. Even where a congregation cannot reflect catholicity among its members because of the makeup of its surrounding population, it can do so by joyfully embracing music, worship patterns, and theological insights from other parts of the church, not as exotic treats or marketing tools but as participation in and witness to the fullness and richness and glory and wealth of the kingdom of God.

Apostolic

In the church's tradition, apostolicity has commonly been understood as obedience to the apostolic mission and the apostolic teaching. Since *apostle* means "sent one," obedience to the apostolic may be understood as fulfilling the Great Commission—a task that was the focus of chapters 7 and 8. So in this chapter I will identify and develop an account of obedience to the apostles' teaching as a

8. Andrew F. Walls, *The Missionary Movement in Christian History: Studies in the Transmission of Faith* (Maryknoll, NY: Orbis, 1996), and *The Cross-Cultural Movement in Modern Missions* (Maryknoll, NY: Orbis, 2002); and Philip Jenkins, *The Next Christendom: The Coming of Global Christianity* (Toronto: Oxford University Press, 2002). My own hope is that the rise of Christianity in the Southern Hemisphere will be something more wonderful than a "new Christendom," since the old Christendom of Europe has left us a legacy that is often to be repented and confessed.

practice of the church.[9] This faithfulness was a mark of the early community of disciples, who "devoted themselves to the apostles' teaching and fellowship, to the breaking of bread and the prayers" (Acts 2:42).

Today the apostles' teaching comes to us through scripture. Our devotion to the teaching of scripture is one form of the church's apostolicity. As we consider scriptural faithfulness as a practice, I will develop an account of biblical interpretation that places it within the context of a social network of relationships gathered around the scripture as a means of life in the kingdom of God. The practice of interpretation that I describe will contrast with the tradition of scholarly interpretation and with the typical practice of Bible study groups of people without training in biblical interpretation—what are often called lay Bible studies.

Both of these approaches have significant limitations. The scholarly tradition restricts biblical interpretation to a group of people with similar skills and training. This training typically provides them with a rather standard set of questions and a method for answering them, even when the answers may be new ones. In this tradition, biblical interpretation often seems to require mastery of a special vocabulary and credentials for admission to a secret club. The questions and arguments often make little connection to the life of the church but seem instead to be part of a self-perpetuating knowledge industry in which only other scholars purchase, read, and talk about the books and articles that are produced. There is something to be said for this tradition, and I have a whole section of my library devoted to these works, which I read with profit, but they do often seem to be quite removed from devotion to the apostles' teaching. But even more significant, this scholarly tradition neglects the wide range of relationships and gifts that make biblical interpretation "apostolic."

9. For many Christians around the world, such as Anglicans and Roman Catholics, the "apostolicity" of the church is marked by "apostolic succession," in which apostolicity is safeguarded by the process of calling a new generation of leaders. Even in these traditions, however, the aim of the process is faithfulness to the apostles' mission and teaching. The differences among the traditions arise from how to remain "apostolic." The argument that I present here about faithfulness to the apostles' teaching applies to all who are members of the one church described earlier in this chapter.

The alternative that many congregations engage in does no better. In this activity, which never reaches the level of *practice*, people gather around a portion of scripture to talk with one another about what the passage means to them or, too often, how it makes them feel or what use they can make of the text. These are understandable expressions of a misdirected and inchoate sense that these texts are connected to the life of the kingdom. But the scholarly tradition is beyond most disciples' attainment, so their quest for life through these texts can be an undisciplined and chaotic mess.

In contrast to these two activities, the scholarly and the populist, the apostolicity of the church guides us to a practice of devotion to the apostles' teaching that recognizes the necessity and role of scripture scholars but places them within the disciple community, not the scholarly guild, for their contributions to and participation in that apostolicity. Similarly, the practice of apostolicity requires the participation of all the gifts of the disciple community but brings discipline and direction to their participation. For the disciple community, the practice of apostolicity in devotion to scripture envisions the community gathered around the text to discern God's speech to it as a guide to faithfully living out and witnessing to the good news of the kingdom.

For scholars, this practice recognizes that their gifts and learning are essential to the right understanding of scripture and discerning its teaching for the community. These contributions include knowledge of the original languages, the cultural context, the history of interpretation, and systematic thinking about biblical teaching. Given the typical scholarly temperament, their contributions may also come through forcing the community to consider various possible meanings and guidance as well as carefulness about words and their nuances. But the practice of the disciple community also requires scholars to participate in the network of relationships that constitute the community. Scholars, in their participation in the church's apostolicity, are responsible to other disciples.

Other disciples (those without scholarly training in the Bible) participate in the apostolicity of the church when they read scripture in the community as an exercise not of personal opinion or feeling but as an exercise of their spiritual gifts. As the community gathers, one person who counsels families is sensitive to dimensions of a text that may not be noticed by the scholar whose reading of the text has been conditioned by other scholars. Or the social worker or the public defender may wrestle with an aspect of the text that is missed by an investment banker or a homemaker, and vice versa.

In this practice, the goal is not to express one's opinion but to see and hear the text with various eyes and ears that are trained to see and hear different things by virtue of temperament, training, and work. As the gifts of the disciple community come together, the voice and guidance of the Spirit may become evident to all. The presence of trained scripture scholars is essential to this practice, whether in the person of a pastor, a lay leader with training, or a written commentary or study guide. The responsibility of the scholar is not to serve as the expert on what the text meant or means but to contribute knowledge of the languages, context, and history, so that the disciple community gathered around the text can together discern the apostles' teaching for them.

When we set it within a teleological context, this practice of the disciple community becomes an embodiment of its apostolicity when the community discerns together the life of the kingdom that they see and hear through devoting themselves to the apostles' teaching. The *telos* of apostolicity is the further faithful participation of the community in the kingdom of God. Since the end is life in the kingdom, apostolicity is obedience to the apostles' teaching. It is not interpreting scripture; rather, apostolicity is, in the marvelous phrase of Nicholas Lash, "performing the Scriptures."

Confession as Practice

The fourfold confession of the church as one, holy, catholic, and apostolic makes sense only within the church's participation in the life of the kingdom. It is in this participation and the *telos* it anticipates that the church's life takes shape. When the church seeks to turn this confession into witness to its own reality, it must engage in lies and illusions. This common sin has often corrupted the church's life and turned it toward self-preservation. But when the severe mercy of God brings discipline, the sanctifying power of the Holy Spirit restores the witness of the church to the kingdom as the church confesses its faith.

10

Suffering as the Power of the Kingdom

At various times in history, teachers of the church have contemplated suffering as one of the marks of the church. But such consideration seems usually to be confined to periods during which the church is actually suffering. When the circumstances pass, so also does the question of suffering as part of the church's life. In this chapter, I will place suffering back on the theological agenda as a *practice* of the church.

By considering suffering as a practice of the church, I intend to remove it from the realm of temporary condition and fix it firmly as a pervasive practice of the church. To do this, I will draw on some concepts that have guided the work I have been doing in this book. But I will also add two more ingredients. First, I will develop my account of suffering through a closer reading of scripture than has been practiced up to this point. I do this because I want to root this difficult practice—suffering—within the primary authority of the church's life. Second, I will develop my account of suffering as reflection on the practice of power in the church. I do this in order to bring into focus the question of power that lurks in the midst of any discussion of practices and to locate the practice of suffering within the life of the kingdom. By locating suffering within the power of the life of the kingdom I hope to maintain a healthy relationship between suffering and power.

The exercise of power in the church is complex and multifaceted. It involves the organization of the church, the leadership of the church, its decision making and the process of communication, along with many other matters. All of these deserve careful attention and faithful practice. In this chapter, I will focus closely on one aspect of power in the church as a way of providing a model for thinking about and living out all practices of power in the life of the church.

Throughout the earlier chapters of this book, the question of power arose regularly. We cannot simply take refuge in powerlessness because the abuse of power is so prevalent in human history, including the life of the church. This, of course, is the temptation—to counter the problems of the corrupt exercise of power by supposing that one can avoid exercising power. As studies of family systems teach us clearly, the claim of powerlessness is itself the exercise of a particular kind of power: it turns others into rescuers and produces and manipulates guilt in those whom we identify as the powerful. In essence we say, "Take pity on us. We are weak; you are strong. It's your responsibility to help us, rescue us, fix us." The same kind of manipulation can occur in other human relationships and activities, where the claim to be a victim may mask the exercise of power.

The proper way to practice power is further complicated by our cultural uncertainties. In modernity, the exercise of power is directed toward establishing individual freedom and determining one's own destiny. In postmodernity, it has no other goal than an arbitrary exercise of power on behalf of my own interest group. That interest group may vary from setting to setting as we live increasingly fragmented lives.

But all these complications do not do away with the fact that power is often abused and many are victims of the unjust exercise of power. If an appeal to "powerlessness" is not the answer to these problems, neither is a refusal to consider the proper practice of power. Nor do the difficulties of our cultural context excuse us from the complex issues of power.

If God has given God's people, the church, a mission, then we must believe that God equips us for accomplishing that mission. And if the kingdom of God is the *telos* of the cosmos in which the church has its life and calling, then the church must acknowledge that it is empowered for that life and calling. The power of the church, then, is its participation in the kingdom of God. When we describe the church's practice of power in its own life and in its mission to the world, we must always seek to bring that understanding and practice into alignment with the kingdom of God.

Spirit

Jesus promises his disciple community that they will receive power:

> He said to them, "Thus it is written, that the Messiah is to suffer and to rise from the dead on the third day, and that repentance and forgiveness of sins is to be proclaimed in his name to all nations, beginning from Jerusalem. You are witnesses of these things. And see, I am sending upon you what my Father promised; so stay here in the city until you have been clothed with power from on high." (Luke 24:46–49)

> "It is not for you to know the times or periods that the Father has set by his own authority. But you will receive power when the Holy Spirit has come upon you; and you will be my witnesses in Jerusalem, in all Judea and Samaria, and to the ends of the earth." (Acts 1:7–8)

> Jesus said to them again, "Peace be with you. As the Father has sent me, so I send you." When he had said this, he breathed on them and said to them, "Receive the Holy Spirit. If you forgive the sins of any, they are forgiven them; if you retain the sins of any, they are retained." (John 20:21–23)

These passages obviously promise power to the disciple community. And that promise is fulfilled at the Feast of Pentecost, when the Holy Spirit comes on the disciples.

The coming of the Holy Spirit to empower the disciples and the Spirit's continuing work have been a source of difference and division in the past. Today, that is much less the case. If we keep our focus on the clear teaching of these passages, we will discover some significant guidance for the practice of power in the church across many traditions.

The coming of the Spirit is, first, the fulfillment of a promise made by Jesus. It is inextricably tied to his identity and work. Indeed, in all of these passages, the empowering gift of the Spirit follows from the commissioning of the disciples. We may say that along with the assignment of the task comes the power to accomplish it. But that introduces too much of a distinction into these passages. The greater truth here is that the life of Christ that they have seen among them will continue as life in them and as the life in which they will live. This life in them is the presence of the Holy Spirit. The disciple community will be witnesses of "these things" because Christ will continue to live in them by the Holy Spirit.[1]

In chapter 7, I argued that the mission of the church is to witness to the kingdom in word and in deed. When the Spirit comes on the disciples, their witness is empowered in word and deed. As Peter preaches on Pentecost, thousands hear the word and begin the journey of discipleship through baptism (Acts 2). This initial witness in word is followed by many more accounts of the disciples' faithful words of witness and the power of those words. The Spirit also empowers the deeds of the disciples as their common life witnesses to "these things" to which Jesus called them:

> All the believers were one in heart and mind. No one claimed that any of their possessions was their own, but they shared everything they had. With great power the apostles continued to testify to the resurrection of the Lord Jesus. And God's grace was so powerfully at work in them all that there were no needy persons among them. (Acts 4:32–34 TNIV)

These practices embody in the disciple community the power of the Spirit as the community bears witness to "these things" to which Jesus called them. They proclaim and perform the life of the kingdom.

But immediately following the declaration of Acts 4, we encounter the story of the unfaithfulness of Ananias and Sapphira. Here is the realism of the New Testament about the exercise of power in

---

1. See the creative, dense, sometimes speculative, always instructive development of this theme in Douglas B. Farrow, *Ascension and Ecclesia: On the Significance of the Doctrine of the Ascension for Ecclesiology and Christian Cosmology* (Grand Rapids: Eerdmans, 1999).

the life of the church, even in times of great faithfulness. So we are again reminded that the Spirit's empowering and the practices that embody that power must be aligned with the kingdom of God to be the way of life. The judgment that falls upon Ananias and Sapphira is the judgment of the one *telos*: if our "life" is not the life of the kingdom, then it is death, not life.

So the power of the Spirit is given to the church so that the church may be aligned with and participate in the kingdom. This power is not the power to accomplish whatever the church may choose. Nor is it the power to sustain the life of the church apart from the kingdom. The power of the Spirit does not confer upon the church status or privilege or blessing, except as the church participates in the kingdom.

As the early disciple community learned that their empowerment was for the sake of witness to the kingdom, they teach us something crucial to the practice of power in the church today. In Acts 5, shortly after the explosive growth of the church and the wonderful description of their common life, we read that

> many signs and wonders were done among the people through the apostles. And they were all together in Solomon's Portico. None of the rest dared to join them, but the people held them in high esteem. Yet more than ever believers were added to the Lord, great numbers of both men and women. (Acts 5:12–14)

This powerful life of the church led to great concern among the high priest and the other Sadducees, so they arrested and jailed the apostles. After the apostles were released by an angel and found once again preaching at the temple, they were once again arrested. At that hearing, Gamaliel, a respected teacher of the law, counseled the Jewish leaders to a kind of pragmatism:

> "Leave these men alone! Let them go! For if their purpose or activity is of human origin, it will fail. But if it is from God, you will not be able to stop these men; you will only find yourselves fighting against God."
>
> His speech persuaded them. They called the apostles in and had them flogged. Then they ordered them not to speak in the name of Jesus, and let them go. (Acts 5:38–40 TNIV)

At this point, "the apostles left the Sanhedrin, rejoicing" (Acts 5:41 TNIV).

I interrupt the story at this point so that we may consider the reasons the apostles have for rejoicing. Their preaching has resulted in the salvation of thousands. The proclamation of the good news at the Feast of Pentecost will result in the message's being carried throughout the empire by the Jews who were visiting Jerusalem for the feast. Many miraculous signs have been performed, and many people have been healed. But as the apostles went on their way rejoicing, we are told that they rejoiced *"because they had been counted worthy of suffering disgrace for the Name"* (Acts 5:41 TNIV).

Power and Suffering

This is the lesson of the early community of disciples: the power of the Spirit is the power to suffer as witnesses to the good news of the kingdom of life in Jesus Christ. This insight is key to the church's practice of power. Power is not the means to avoid suffering or protect oneself or one's community from suffering. Nor is the suffering of the church a sign of our powerlessness. Nor is suffering in itself a good. Rather, when the church is empowered to live by the kingdom of God in a world that is in rebellion against that kingdom, suffering is the consequence of faithful witness.

Paul understood this in his own apostolic ministry. After his ministry that established the church in Corinth, he was challenged by some who called themselves "super-apostles." In effect they seem to have been saying, "Paul may be an apostle, but we're *super-apostles.*" Clearly issues of identity, authority, and power are intertwined in this challenge. Paul met the challenge on two bases: his preaching of the cross of Christ and his own suffering. As studies have shown, Paul is deploying some sophisticated rhetoric in defense of his ministry and the gospel he proclaims. But in the midst of the rhetoric he is also identifying the power of ministry and mission in relation to the cross of Christ and Paul's personal history.

By drawing on the cross of Christ, Paul reminds us that the empowering of the Spirit makes us witnesses to Jesus Christ, whose way of life led to his crucifixion. Certainly the resurrection of Jesus

Christ makes the Holy Spirit available to us, but the Spirit empowers us to follow Christ, to live in the kingdom, in an age that is in rebellion against Christ and God's kingdom. The proclamation of the cross of Christ declares that this age is upside down; this age gets life exactly wrong, leading to death.

The power of the cross is lived out in Paul's own life history. When he finally confronts the super-apostles, he lays out his own apostolic credentials:

> Are they ministers of Christ? I am talking like a madman—I am a better one: with far greater labors, far more imprisonments, with countless floggings, and often near death. Five times I have received from the Jews the forty lashes minus one. Three times I was beaten with rods. Once I received a stoning. Three times I was shipwrecked; for a night and a day I was adrift at sea; on frequent journeys, in danger from rivers, danger from bandits, danger from my own people, danger from Gentiles, danger in the city, danger in the wilderness, danger at sea, danger from false brothers and sisters. (2 Cor. 11:23–26)

In this passage Paul weaves together natural dangers and human dangers that he faced. Although not all these dangers were directed toward him because he was a disciple of Jesus Christ, he faced them because of the life to which he was called in the kingdom. And of course, Paul almost never traveled alone, so these dangers were also faced by the community of disciples with whom he ministered.

Paul talks about his weakness in this context, but in the rhetorical situation Paul is challenging the Corinthian church to revise its definitions of power and weakness in light of Christ's cross and the kingdom of God. What counted as power for the super-apostles was not the power of the Spirit to make us witnesses to Christ in this age. Yes, Christ is risen, but this age is not yet judged and the kingdom is not yet fully present. Therefore, in this age following Christ means suffering. That is the church's power by the Spirit.

Suffering for Christ

When the power of suffering is set in the context of following Christ, we are guarded from valuing suffering for its own sake. Suffering, in itself, is not good. If it were, then a vision of everlasting life as a life of suffering would be a rather perverse understanding. The suffering that is empowered by the Spirit is not natural to the life of the kingdom. It is natural only to the life of the kingdom *lived in this rebellious age.* It is life lived in territory that is occupied and for the moment ruled by death. In the age that is coming in the kingdom of God, suffering will be no more because this rebellious age will have no more power.

Too often accounts of the Christian life choose between a "theology of glory," thought to reflect the primacy of the resurrection as the model for Christian life, and a "theology of suffering," thought to reflect the cross as the model for Christian life. In reality, the choice is a false one. Christian life is empowered by the Holy Spirit, whose presence is enabled by Christ's resurrection. But that resurrection life is lived in a world ruled temporarily by the alien power of death. So the power of the disciple community is the power to live by the resurrection in the midst of death and the power to bear faithfully the suffering that results. In a classic passage, John Howard Yoder teaches that "the believer's cross is not some illness or the cranky neighbor or the difficult boss. Rather, the believer's cross is the natural consequence of living by love in a world that crucifies love. It is the price of our social non-conformity."[2]

This social nonconformity is not a trivial strategy of taking our cues from the world: observe what the world does and do the opposite. No, the social nonconformity of the church is teleological. The church's vision is fixed not on the world but on the kingdom of God, in which it has its life by the power of the Spirit. This vision of the kingdom guides the life of the church. That vision is learned through the disciplined practices that I have identified in this book and many more practices that may also be proper to the church's life in the kingdom.

The "kingdom conformity" that embodies social nonconformity and leads to suffering may be seen in many instances of the persecuted church around the world. In many cases, avoiding the suffering of persecution would be a relatively simple matter of conforming to

2. John Howard Yoder, *The Politics of Jesus: Vicit Agnus Noster*, 2nd ed. (Grand Rapids: Eerdmans, 1994), 97.

the demands of political and economic powers that are in rebellion against the kingdom. In North America, suffering in conformity to the kingdom takes place more among Christian communities on the margin of our society, but it should be much more widespread. The historic peace churches of the Mennonites, Church of the Brethren, and Quakers, and other Christian communities that join them regard their pacifism as participation in the kingdom. However one may judge the question of Christian pacifism, these traditions provide an example of social nonconformity in witness to the kingdom—a nonconformity historically leading to suffering that makes sense only in light of the kingdom. In a similar way, Christian communities that regard life with the poor and oppressed as the call of the kingdom also represent the teleological suffering of the kingdom. These examples remind us that the suffering as a practice of the church must always be judged in relation to its participation in the life of the kingdom.

The Suffering and Power of the Church Today

Either the church, as the people of God, suffers at the hands of the world because of our faithfulness to the kingdom, or we suffer at the hands of God because of our unfaithfulness. To be chosen as the people of God is to be chosen for the purpose of bearing witness to the work of Christ in the world. Both forms of suffering fulfill that mission.

In different parts of the world today, the church knows different forms of that suffering. In European cultures (including North America), it seems to me that the church is beginning to suffer under God's judgment. We have lost our way; we no longer live by the *telos* of the cosmos. Our life may look rich and vital, but it is not the life of the kingdom. This book is in part my modest contribution to redirecting the church toward its *telos*, its true life. The church lives not for itself or its nation but for Christ in the world. In this context, the church must hear the promise made to God's people in the Old Testament: "If my people, who are called by my name, will humble themselves and pray and seek my face and turn from their wicked ways, then I will hear from heaven, and I will forgive their sin and will heal their land" (2 Chron. 7:14 TNIV). This is the call to God's people, the church, today, not a nation-state. May the church hear and repent.

In many parts of the world outside European cultures, the church knows the suffering that comes at the hands of the world. Persecution and death face Christ's disciples daily. In these places, the words of Jesus bring hope:

> Blessed are those who are persecuted for righteousness' sake, for theirs is the kingdom of heaven.
> Blessed are you when people revile you and persecute you and utter all kinds of evil against you falsely on my account. Rejoice and be glad, for your reward is great in heaven, for in the same way they persecuted the prophets who were before you. (Matt. 5:10–12)

This passage summarizes beautifully the meaning of the practice of the power of the Spirit for suffering in faithfulness to the kingdom.

In the midst of this long description of suffering as a mark of the church, we must not lose sight of the power that enables the joyful bearing of suffering and the blessedness of the disciple community. The suffering of the disciple community as we are empowered by the Spirit is not a pathological celebration of suffering. Nor is it the manipulative delight in weakness that Friedrich Nietzsche so despised. Rather, the suffering of the disciple community is the practice of the power of life in a world that loves the power of death. The power that sent Jesus to the cross and raised him from the dead is the same power that conquers death and will one day end its reign of terror. When the church refuses to worship death and its power, the church bears faithful witness to the greater power of the life of love—when that life is our participation in the love of God that sent Jesus Christ to the cross for the redemption of the world.

141

Appendix

Practicing Church

Evangelical Ecclesiologies at the End of Modernity

(Francis Schaeffer, Charles Colson,
Rick Warren, and Brian McLaren)

(An earlier version of the following was read at the Wheaton Theology Conference, April 2003. The text below is a revision of that essay as it was published as chapter 3 of the volume from the conference: Daniel J. Treier and Mark A. Husbands, eds., *Community of the Word* [Downers Grove: InterVarsity Press, 2004], 59–75. I have included it to show how the insights and arguments that I have been pursuing here might apply to other practitioners of church. Reprinted here with permission.)

One natural place to turn for evangelical ecclesiology is to evangelical theologians or to those nonevangelical theologians to whom evangelicals often look. So we might explore the work of Carl Henry, Donald Bloesch, Stanley Grenz, or Veli-Matti Karkainnen. Or we might examine Karl Barth, Wolfhart Pannenberg, Jürgen Moltmann, T. F. Torrance, George Lindbeck, or Ephraim Radner. Any one of these projects would be worthwhile and fruitful. But none would get us close to "evangelical ecclesiology."

In an article published in *Christian Century*, Jackson Carroll reports that a survey of the reading habits of evangelical clergy reveals that no theologian is among their favorite authors, no theology is among their most recently read books, and no theological journal is among their frequent reading.[1] To explore evangelical ecclesiology, we must turn to more popular authors, who tend to be other pastors and practitioners of church leadership, not theologians located in the academy, not even the evangelical academy.

Of course, *evangelical* is an equivocal term. It may be used as John Webster uses it:

> The word evangelical is not used here as a term of discrimination (over against, for example, catholic), but in a more primary sense. An evangelical theology is one which is evoked, governed and judged by the gospel. In this sense, evangelical is simply equivalent to Christian; all Christian theology, whatever its tradition, is properly speaking evangelical in that it is determined by and responsible to the good news of Jesus Christ.[2]

This is an entirely defensible and even commendable use of *evangelical* that I also endorse. However, *evangelical* may also be used to refer to an evangelical subculture, that much-studied group whose identity is still essentially contested. This latter use of *evangelical* is the one governing my investigation of evangelical ecclesiologies, though at the conclusion of this essay I will make some suggestions about "evangelical" ecclesiology in the former sense.

To explore evangelical ecclesiology at the end of modernity, I will explore the ecclesiology implicit and explicit in four popular authors whose evangelical identity is unquestioned: Francis Schaeffer, Charles Colson, Rick Warren, and Brian McLaren. The works of these authors spans four decades and ministries that represent different institutional settings. I will begin with a survey that seeks to be descriptive of these works. Then I will propose some identity markers

1. Jackson W. Carroll, "Pastors' Picks: What Clergy Are Reading," *Christian Century*, August 23, 2003, available online: http://www.pulpitandpew.duke.edu/pastorspicks.html.

2. John Webster, *Word and Church: Essays in Christian Dogmatics* (Edinburgh: T and T Clark, 2001), 191.

for evangelical ecclesiology and advocate a normative understanding of evangelical ecclesiology as missional and improvisational.

Francis Schaeffer

For many in my generation, the work of Francis Schaeffer was a passage into a larger intellectual world. In many of his writings, Schaeffer placed the church front and center.[3] In these works Schaeffer develops an explicit ecclesiology, though not in the standard form of systematic theology.

In *The Church at the End of the Twentieth Century*, Schaeffer begins with a cultural analysis that condenses the argument of his earlier books *Escape from Reason* and *The God Who Is There*. As Schaeffer himself notes, this repetition reflects his commitment to rooting the church in a particular time and place (5). This cultural critique then becomes the basis for an ecclesiology that recognizes the existence of "co-belligerents" with the church in the course of history, the centrality of truth in preaching and in practice, the necessity of "the orthodoxy of community," and the New Testament teaching on "form and freedom" of the church (59).

In his sensitivity to the cultural situation, Schaeffer recognizes that the church's voice on injustice or politics may blend with others. In these cases, Schaeffer wants the church to be clear that these other voices are not allies but cobelligerents. He is, of course, famously concerned for "true truth" in the context of late modernity and the subjectivism that he perceived there. But that concern for truth is not limited to propositions for Schaeffer; it extends as well to practice. This theme was perhaps Schaeffer's most significant contribution as he pushed the evangelical church beyond its comfortable practices into a hospitable and compassionate Christianity that welcomed "others"—members of racial minorities, drug users, dropouts, and misfits.[4]

---

3. I will refer parenthetically to the following books by Francis A. Schaeffer: *The Church at the End of the Twentieth Century* (Downers Grove, IL: InterVarsity Press, 1970); *The Church Before the Watching World: A Practical Ecclesiology* (Downers Grove, IL: InterVarsity Press, 1971); *True Spirituality* (Wheaton, IL: Tyndale House, 1971).

4. See Schaeffer, *Church*, 105–12, and *True Spirituality*, 168–71.

Schaeffer wrestled with two tensions in his work. One was the balance of form and freedom, in which he sought to establish the authoritative guidance of the New Testament teaching alongside the transformations necessary to the fulfillment of the mission of the church as he saw it in a particular cultural moment. The other, more difficult tension was the challenge of balancing the call to visible purity with the "mark of the Christian"—love.[5] In the midst of our remembering, critically and appreciatively, Schaeffer's "propositional apologetics," we must also remember that he calls "observable love" the "final apologetic": "The world . . . should be able to observe that we do love each other. Our love must have a form that the world may observe; it must be seeable" (*Mark*, 34).

Although my purpose here is not to evaluate, even briefly, Schaeffer's ministry as a whole, his achievements in evangelical ecclesiology can be well understood only against the backdrop of his own militantly separatist and fundamentalist heritage. Under the pressure of a missionary situation and in faithfulness to the gospel, Schaeffer develops an ecclesiology that goes beyond his own heritage. In Schaffer's work we find someone who engages the world as the place of mission, not as something to be repelled or walled off. Of course, he is not the first or only evangelical to do this, but his writings develop and popularize an evangelical engagement with culture out of concern for the church's mission.[6] Second, in a missionary situation, Schaeffer engages issues about the oneness, holiness, catholicity, and apostolicity of the church that were seldom problems for the fundamentalist tradition in which he was rooted. This wrestling gave rise to some unresolved tensions in Schaeffer's ecclesiology that continue in some evangelical ecclesiology today but drop away from others. Those tensions include the problem of critically engaging the culture without being compromised or co-opted and giving an account of the creedal affirmations that maintains the uniqueness of evangelical identity.

5. *The Mark of the Christian* was first included in *Church at the End of the Twentieth Century* and then published in the same year (1970) as a separate work.

6. Carl Henry and others had already initiated this movement of serious cultural engagement. Schaeffer does so as an evangelist and popularizer rooted in the church, not the academy.

Charles Colson

Twenty-two years after Schaeffer's *Church at the End of the Twentieth Century*, Charles Colson and Ellen Vaughn published *The Body: Being Light in Darkness*.[7] Colson and Vaughn retrieve much that is characteristic of Schaeffer's earlier work.[8] They begin with cultural analysis to root their ecclesiology in a particular time and place. They have the same concern for cobelligerents, truth, and community that characterized Schaeffer's work.[9] But in the midst of this retrieval, they extend their ecclesiology into three additional areas.

First, they make significantly more use of church history than does Schaeffer. True, Schaeffer provided a historical narrative, but it was done primarily to show the course of culture as it rebelled against God. In *Being the Body*, the authors interweave exemplary stories from the history of the church to display the roots of our life and to guide our present and future life. The message of these examples is that we have much to learn from the past centuries.

Second, the authors broaden the identity of the church they address and learn from. The global vision of the church that they display contributes wonderfully to enlarging the world of North American Christians, but they also enlarge the boundaries of evangelical Christianity beyond Schaeffer to include Catholic Christianity.

7. Charles W. Colson with Ellen Santilli Vaughn, *The Body: Being Light in the Darkness* (Dallas: Word, 1992). An updated, post–9/11 version of the book has been issued as *Being the Body* (Dallas: W Publishing, 2003). This new edition responds to 9/11 and diagnoses the early response from the church in the United States as moving toward Christian faithfulness, then changing direction. It uses this turn of events to call once more for greater faithfulness in the church.

8. This relationship between Colson's work and Schaeffer's could be pursued at many levels. For its clearest expression, compare Charles Colson and Nancy Pearcey, *How Now Shall We Live?* (Wheaton, IL: Tyndale House, 1999), which is dedicated to Francis Schaeffer, with Schaeffer's own *How Shall We Then Live?* (Westchester, IL: Crossway, 1983).

9. Although it is not central to my concern in this chapter, I must register my opposition to the use of "worldview language" by many evangelicals, including Schaeffer, Colson, and Vaughn. This language is pervasive and formative. I may identify my opposition cryptically by noting that the church does not proclaim or live by a "worldview." We proclaim news of God's work of redemption centered in Jesus Christ and continuing throughout history. Christianity is not a set of ideas; it is the power of God in Christ to redeem the world. And we live in this redemption by the power and guidance of the Holy Spirit. My late professor of theology Klaus Bockmuehl first taught me that worldview language "will not do."

And in these examples, they are recognizing not mere cobelligerents but allies with whom we are to practice visible unity in action.[10]

The third change that Colson and Vaughn reflect in their work is a thicker account of the call to justice. This concern for justice is present in Schaeffer's work, but in a thinner, nascent way. Colson and Vaughn develop it in detail and make it much more central to their account of "being light in darkness."[11]

Finally, we should note that the authors begin with the overarching concern that the church lives *Coram Deo*. As they move into their exposition, they assert that "what the church needs most desperately is holy fear. The passion to please God more than the culture and the community in which we spend these few, short years" (28). And they note early on the discomfort they may cause as a result of their broad commitment to "one holy catholic and apostolic church" (14).

In *Being the Body*, the authors, perhaps consciously, follow the outline of the creed. In part 1, "What Is the Church?" they exposit the oneness of the church. In part 2, "The Church against the World," the themes are really drawn from the church's holiness and catholicity (though less from the latter). Finally, in part 3, "The Church in the World," the apostolicity of the church guides the equipping of the saints for ministry and mission.

Rick Warren

The purpose-driven phenomenon is well known in North American Christianity and beyond. *The Purpose-Driven Life* has sold more than fifteen million copies, and its success has picked up Warren's earlier book, *The Purpose-Driven Church*, and given it greater influence than it had on its initial release.[12]

10. Charles Colson is, of course, one of the architects of *Evangelicals and Catholics Together*.

11. "Being light in darkness" is given even more prominence in the revised edition by the rearrangement of some chapters so that the book concludes with chapters on "Lighting the Night" and "Go Light Your Candle." This rearrangement reflects the authors' response after 9/11, but it does seem to lose some of the firm foundation of the previous edition, which concluded with "The Fear of the Lord Is the Beginning" and "Coram Deo."

12. Rick Warren, *The Purpose-Driven Life* (Grand Rapids: Zondervan, 2002), and *The Purpose-Driven Church: Growth without Compromising Your Message and Mission* (Grand Rapids: Zondervan, 1995).

In *The Purpose-Driven Church*, we move into a world very different from that of Schaeffer, Colson, and Vaughn. Their ecclesiology is close to the surface of their work, and the attentive reader can discern the guidance that they are drawing from Christian tradition. It is difficult to discern any ecclesiology that guides Warren's book. This absence—or perhaps less tendentiously, this silence—implies a number of things.

Before turning to the implications of that silence, a brief digression is warranted, because the very style of Warren's book shapes its impact on readers. Warren's work is very simply written and organized. The chapters consist mostly of bold headings and italicized statements that are also typically numbered. Text that follows these headings is repetitive, and sidebars and boxes highlight portions of the text. This style carries over into content. The book consists of a compilation of scripture verses, slogans, and good advice. None of this is bad in itself, but it does beg the question of ecclesiology.

As I noted, Warren's ecclesiology may only be discerned, if at all, almost entirely in the silences. So with some caution I will argue that Warren's work reflects the following characteristics.

First, the absence of any critical examination of culture implies that the relationship between the church and culture is unproblematic. The book does argue for cultural sensitivity but only as a means of communicating the message to a target audience. Culture is not an impediment to faithful discipleship except insofar as we fail to understand the culture and thus fail to communicate and persuade. Warren's ecclesiology is silent on "the world" as a theological challenge.

Second, the reader looks in vain for evidence in this book that reflects the oneness, holiness, and catholicity of the church. In this respect, Warren's ecclesiology shows no concern for the particularities of time and place as a theological problem. Even the theme of apostolicity, which a sympathetic reader might discern in the commitment to scripture and discipleship, loses its significance when it is detached from any particularities, when it lacks content. A cultural and historical naiveté runs throughout the book. This naiveté allows the author to make many assertions of the following nature: "We should never criticize any method that God is blessing" (156), as if "God's blessing" were itself an unproblematic term.

Finally, the silences in Warren's work leave untouched the individualism of North American culture. Yes, *The Purpose-Driven Life* begins by asserting that "it's not about you." But the overall message of the book is that it *is* about you and your fulfillment. The ecclesiology implied in this book is fully expressed in the earlier book, where the church is instrumental to the fulfillment of individuals. Warren himself supports this conclusion, perhaps inadvertently, when he asserts in other writings and in interviews that his proposal is an "Intel chip" that can be inserted into many different settings.

I have written the foregoing lines knowing the sales figures for Warren's books, his widespread impact on pastors, and the testimony of many to fulfilling lives as a result of his books and seminars. But I am troubled by his unproblematic approach to our cultural and ecclesiological situation. Perhaps the popularity of his books indicates a movement of the Spirit. But it may also be a reflection of how well his work reflects back to our culture its aspirations and "values." I pray it is the former; I fear it is the latter.

Brian McLaren

In Brian McLaren's work, we encounter an innovative format and creative thinking that nevertheless stand in continuity with the works we have already examined. Two of McLaren's books, *A New Kind of Christian* and *The Story We Find Ourselves In,* are fictional tales that present his vision for Christianity and the church.[13] Our focus here will be on his more expositional ecclesiology, *The Church on the Other Side.*[14] McLaren's format is similar to Warren's, with its bold text, italics, and constant numbering, but its ecclesiology is significantly closer to Schaeffer, Colson, and Vaughn.[15]

13. Brian D. McLaren, *A New Kind of Christian: A Tale of Two Friends on a Spiritual Journey* (San Francisco: Jossey-Bass, 2001), and *The Story We Find Ourselves In: Further Adventures of a New Kind of Christian* (San Francisco: Jossey-Bass, 2003).

14. Brian D. McLaren, *The Church on the Other Side: Doing Ministry in the Postmodern Matrix* (Grand Rapids: Zondervan, 2000). This is a revised and expanded edition of *Reinventing Your Church.*

15. While McLaren's ecclesiology is similar to those of Schaeffer, Colson, and Vaughn, his estimate of our cultural situation differs. Where the others draw significantly on modernity for their understanding of truth and still have a lingering dependence on the Constantinian arrangement, McLaren draws on postmodernity. For a conversation between McLaren and

McLaren is sensitive to the cultural context for communicating faith, but also recognizes, to a degree, "the world" as opposition to the church and gospel. For example, in an early chapter of *The Church on the Other Side*, McLaren tells us that his first writing of the chapter "implied that God, like any good modern, is interested only in individuals" (34). He calls us to enlarge our vision of reality beyond the individual. In this he perceives the cultural challenge of modernity. He then spends much of the book identifying the "postmodern matrix" of culture in which we are increasingly moving. The critical edge he exhibits toward modernity dulls quite a bit as he turns his attention to the postmodern. His approach to postmodernity begins to resemble Warren's approach to modernity. Just as modernity is unproblematic for Warren, postmodernity appears to be unproblematic for McLaren.

Moving on from cultural context, McLaren exhibits an ecclesiology concerned with oneness in his call to "trade-up" from traditions to tradition. In calling us to move beyond the narrow traditions of denominations or even transdenominational movements such as evangelicalism, McLaren directs evangelicals toward a concern for the oneness of the church. He also displays great concern for the apostolicity of the church in vigorous advocacy of the mission of the church. However, the pursuit of apostolic mission threatens to overwhelm any consideration of apostolic faithfulness. That is, where Schaeffer wrestled with "form and freedom" in relation to the teaching of the New Testament, McLaren displays no such anxiety. His eighth strategy advises, "Abandon Structures As They Are Outgrown," by "adopt[ing] a new paradigm for church structure that allows for routine reengineering based on changes in size, constituency, resources, and strategy" (95). This advice is unaccompanied by any cautions, warnings, or limitations drawn from apostolic tradition.

Similarly, the ecclesiology conveyed by holiness and catholicity is muted at best in McLaren's work. There is little to nothing about the

---

Colson, see www.anewkindofchristian.com. For my own evaluation of these complicated matters, see Jonathan R. Wilson, *Gospel Virtues: Practicing Faith, Hope, and Love in Uncertain Times* (Downers Grove, IL: InterVarsity Press, 1998) for a running critique of modernity and postmodernity, and *Living Faithfully in a Fragmented World: Lessons for the Church from MacIntyre's "After Virtue"* (Valley Forge, PA: Trinity Press International, 1997) for an account of church-world relations.

church set apart or called out as a people by God. McLaren pursues a vigorous critique of the relationship between modernity and Christianity, but even here the problem with modernity seems to be less that modernity is an expression of "the world" and more that it is passé and thus any ministry that presumes the culture of modernity will be outdated. But even more significant than the absence of the "set-apartness" of the church is the absence of its set-apartness *to God*. In contrast to Colson and Vaughn, who begin and end their ecclesiology with the fear of the Lord, McLaren's ecclesiology seems driven by the fear of irrelevance. Now, if the church has been called out by God to live for the sake of the world, then irrelevance is a form of unfaithfulness. But fear of irrelevance is not the foundation of ecclesiology, the fear of the Lord is.

Evangelical Ecclesiology: Improvisational or Instrumental?

The preceding expositions do not form an unbroken record of family descent or a coherent narrative of continuity and development. What the preceding exposition provides is some basis for a thesis about evangelical ecclesiology that may be able to guide us into the future.

Both the best and the worst of evangelical ecclesiology are rooted in the passionate evangelical commitment to mission. This engenders flexibility in evangelical ecclesiology that contributes significantly to the accusation that evangelicals do not have an ecclesiology. We do, but our ecclesiology is so flexible that it is difficult at times to identify an effective one.

Of course, there are times—too many of them—when ecclesiology has been entirely abandoned in favor of a mission. By this I mean that no critical reflection is taking place on the mission and its attainment. As a result, the life of the church has no implicit or explicit roots in the work of the triune God. At this point the church easily and inevitably becomes instrumental to something other than the mission given by God. Examples from history are many; examples closer to our time, also numerous, are also more controversial.

What we evangelicals (as a subculture) need is an evangelical ecclesiology, an account of the church that holds us accountable to the gospel. Called into being by the good news of Jesus Christ and empowered for witness to that gospel, the evangelical church needs to maintain a *missional* ecclesiology, with its commitment to mission and concomitant flexibility, while also remaining faithful to our commission. The best way to describe this and equip ourselves for faithful flexibility is to add to our missional ecclesiology an *improvisational* ecclesiology.[16] When evangelical ecclesiology is improvisational, it enables the church to fulfill its mission in changing circumstances.[17] It is wrong to think of faithful and unfaithful improvisation or successful and unsuccessful improvisation. Faithful and successful improvisation is, simply, improvisation.

The strength of evangelicalism is its willingness to adapt its practices to the demands of Christian mission. The weakness is its willingness to neglect our identity within the people of God. An improvisational ecclesiology recognizes the demands of adaptation and faithfulness and commits us to both. We must learn properly to confess in word and deed that the church is one, holy, catholic, and apostolic. But what those mean in particular times and places requires discernment under the guidance of the Spirit.

If an attempt at improvisation is unfaithful or unsuccessful, it does not attain the status of improvisation. Rather it becomes *instrumental*. When evangelical ecclesiology is instrumental, it fails to enable the church to fulfill its mission in changing circumstances. Such instrumental failure may take place when we resist change and

16. The argument of this essay had begun to form when I read the following statement, which brought my thoughts into sharp focus and encouraged me: "Many Protestant evangelicals are convinced that structures of institutional unity must remain open to improvisation." See Carl E. Braaten and Robert W. Jenson, eds., *In One Body through the Cross*, Princeton Proposal for Christian Unity, A Call to the Churches from an Ecumenical Study Group (Grand Rapids: Eerdmans, 2003), 17. After completing this essay I discovered the use of similar terms in a different context but applied to the church in Mary McClintock Fulkerson, "'They Will Know We Are Christians by Our Regulated Improvisation': Ecclesial Hybridity and the Unity of the Church," in *The Blackwell Companion to Postmodern Theology*, ed. Graham Ward (Oxford: Blackwell, 2001), 265–79.

17. I cannot develop an argument here for improvisational ecclesiology. If I were to do so, I imagine two lines of argument. One would depend upon a proper understanding of the kingdom-church-world relations that I describe in pt. 3 of Jonathan R. Wilson, *God So Loved the World: A Christology for Disciples* (Grand Rapids: Baker, 2001). The other line would recount the improvisations of Israel as the people of God in the Old Testament and, since the coming of Jesus, in the continuing history of the Jews.

cling to past forms, or it may take place when we embrace change that disconnects the church from its life source.

In this light, the preceding exposition gives us examples of improvisational and instrumental ecclesiologies. In my judgment, the ecclesiologies of Francis Schaeffer, Charles Colson, and Ellen Vaughn are examples of improvisational ecclesiology. The ecclesiology of Rick Warren is instrumental. And the ecclesiology of Brian McLaren is a still-developing attempt at improvisation. In the last case, I would hope to see further work along the way. To continue with imagery drawn from jazz, McLaren's session in the studio has developed some promising possibilities, but more rehearsal is needed. McLaren's ecclesiology is a work in progress. In a word, it is—well, emerging.

With these admittedly strong and unargued claims before us, we are ready to take one more step—to ask, what contributes to ecclesiological improvisation? Just as jazz requires certain skills, training, and gifts, so also does, may I say it, church jazz. In this case, improvisational ecclesiology depends on some tacit dimensions that are difficult to identify and are acquired through apprenticeship and practice combined with spiritual gifts. But in addition to these intangibles, there are some clearly identifiable characteristics.

Ecclesiological improvisation is most clearly enabled by submission to the greater reality of the kingdom of God. All of our improvisers acknowledge this, though some aspects of the kingdom are muted in McLaren's work. This submission to the kingdom is taught by the tradition through the language of one, holy, catholic, and apostolic. These characteristics, rightly understood, relate the church rightly to its mission in the world and enable improvisation. Learning the language and practices of unity, holiness, catholicity, and apostolicity gives us the skills and practices to adapt creatively, respond imaginatively, and perform faithfully in the midst of the changing culture of particular times and places.

Name and Subject Index

Scripture Index